THE Women's World Cup 2019 Book

Shane Stay

THE WOMEN'S
WORLD CUP
2019
BOOK

Everything You Need to Know About the Soccer World Cup

Meyer & Meyer Sport

British Library Cataloguing in Publication Data
A catalogue record for this book is available from the British Library

THE Women's World Cup 2019 Book
Maidenhead: Meyer & Meyer Sport (UK) Ltd., 2019
ISBN: 978-1-78255-192-8

© 2019 by Meyer & Meyer Sport (UK) Ltd.
Aachen, Auckland, Beirut, Cairo, Cape Town, Dubai, Hägendorf, Hong Kong, Indianapolis,
Manila, New Delhi, Singapore, Sydney, Tehran, Vienna

Member of the World Sports Publishers' Association (WSPA) www.w-s-p-a.org
Printed by C-M Books, Ann Arbor, MI, USA
ISBN: 978-1-78255-192-8
Email: info@m-m-sports.com
www.thesportspublisher.com

CONTENTS

Contents

CHAMPIONS DE LA COUPE DU MON

E DU MONDE FÉMININE DE LA **FIFA**, CANADA 2015™

INTRODUCTION TO
THE WORLD CUP

The illustrious 2019 FIFA Women's World Cup in France will go down as one of the best ever. All of the elite women's teams from around the world are gathered for an ultimate showdown to see who will be number one. Leading the pack this year are the United States, Germany, Canada, France, and England.

The United States is the defending champ, with three titles under its belt, and it hopes to add a fourth. Will the US end this tournament with an astounding fourth World Cup title? If they can do it, the United States women will be the first to reach four titles, but there are many strong teams looking for their chances to win.

Germany, currently ranked number two in the world by FIFA, will have something to say about it. Should Germany win the title, it would be their third. And let's not forget about Japan. The Japanese came in second in the 2015 World Cup, and prior to that it was coming off of its first World Cup title from 2011. Japan, Germany, Canada, France, England, Norway, Brazil, and so many others are lined up to make history. But only one team will emerge a champion. And what better place to host a World Cup than France?

From around the world, every type of media—newspapers, magazines, TV, social media—will be covering the Women's World Cup in France. And don't forget the tourists who travel from all around the globe, just to catch a glimpse of the stars in action.

All the beauty of this history-making tournament is about to unfold. Everything is lined up. The excitement couldn't be greater. We'll get into the history and other interesting facts about the World Cup later in the book, but first, let's meet the teams!

THE GROUPS

GROUP A

France
South Korea
Norway
Nigeria

France has the best chance to win this group, considering it's the host nation. Though watch out for South Korea and Norway. In past years, Norway has been a strong force in women's soccer. It's a team that will definitely push for a run into the second round. Nigeria will play the role of underdog, and it should be an interesting team to watch in this respect; keep an eye on surprising upsets from the Nigerians.

France
Top Player: Amandine Henry
Coach: Corinne Diacre

South Korea
Top Player: Ji Soyun
Coach: Yoon Deokyeo

Norway
Top Player: Maren Mjelde
Coach: Martin Sjogren

Nigeria
Top Player: Asisat Oshoala
Coach: Thomas Dennerby

GROUP B

Germany
China
Spain
South Africa

Germany, by far, is the favorite; however, China should be strong. Don't forget, China had a phenomenal team in the 1999 World Cup where it lost in penalty kicks to the United States. Granted this tournament happened 20 years ago, but still China has the legacy which carries over and transcends time psychologically. Spain might have a few tricks up its sleeve; keep an eye on them for a possible move into the second round. South Africa—not a well-known team in women's soccer—will definitely have to pull off some spectacular performances for a chance to move out of the group.

Germany
Top Player: Dzsenifer Marozsan
Coach: Martina Voss-Tecklenburg

China
Top Player: Li Ying
Coach: Jia Xiuquan

Spain
Top Player: Irene Paredes
Coach: Jorge Vilda

South Africa
Top Player: Janine van Wyk
Coach: Desiree Ellis

GROUP C

Australia
Italy
Brazil
Jamaica

Australia will be a tough team to beat, whereas Italy should be competitive, and Brazil should definitely get out of this group. Jamaica, on the other hand, might have some difficulty.

Australia
Top Player: Sam Kerr
Coach: Alen Stajcic

Italy
Top Player: Barbara Bonansea
Coach: Milena Bertolini

Brazil
Top Player: Marta
Coach: Vadao

Jamaica
Top Player: Jody Brown
Coach: Hue Menzies

GROUP D

England
Scotland
Argentina
Japan

This is an interesting group. England seems like the favorite and for all intents and purposes *probably is the favorite*. Though things might get more interesting as the group progresses, and don't be surprised to see a free for all as each team tries to secure a place in the second round. It could come down to the wire with Scotland, Argentina, and Japan, making this group very exciting to watch.

England
Top Player: Fran Kirby
Coach: Phil Neville

Scotland
Top Player: Kim Little
Coach: Shelley Kerr

Argentina
Top Player: Estefania Banini
Coach: Carlos Borrello

Japan
Top Player: Mana Iwabuchi
Coach: Asako Takakura-Takemoto

GROUP E

Canada
Cameroon
New Zealand
The Netherlands

One would venture to say this is an easy group for Canada. The question remains: Which team other than Canada will move into the second round? Cameroon, New Zealand, and the Netherlands will each have a strong opportunity to out-play one another for a bid at the elimination rounds. Then again, Canada might not be the overall favorite, and it may have more of a challenge than you would think.

Canada
Top Player: Christine Sinclair
Coach: Kenneth Heiner-Moller

Cameroon
Top Player: Gabrielle Onguene
Coach: Joseph Ndoko

New Zealand
Top Player: Ali Riley
Coach: Tom Sermanni

The Netherlands
Top Player: Lieke Martens
Coach: Sarina Wiegman

GROUP F

The United States
Thailand
Chile
Sweden

The United States is clearly the favorite. Keep an eye on the interesting battles between Thailand, Chile, and Sweden for second place. Having said that, Sweden is likely going to finish in second place.

The United States
Top Player: Tobin Heath
Coach: Jill Ellis

Thailand
Top Player: Kanjana Sungngoen
Coach: Nuengruethai Sathongwien

Chile
Top Player: Christiane Endler
Coach: Jose Letelier

Sweden
Top Player: Stina Blackstenius
Coach: Peter Gerhardsson

FIFA announced the draw for the groups on December 8, 2018. Andrew Keh of *The New York Times* wrote, "At a glitzy ceremony Saturday night at La Seine Musicale, a performing arts venue in the western suburbs of Paris, the tournament's 24 teams were placed into four pots based on their world rankings and then drawn into one of six groups. With the exception of Europe, which has the most teams in the field (nine), countries from the same confederation could not be drawn into the same group."[1]

AN IN-DEPTH LOOK AT THE TEAMS OF THE 2019 WOMEN'S WORLD CUP

UNITED STATES

Twitter @ussoccer_wnt
World Cup titles: 3
North American Championships: 8

Known for:
Three World Cup titles
The 1999 World Cup
Strong teams
Very passionate fans
Exciting games
Mia Hamm
Michelle Akers
Kristine Lilly
Julie Foudy
Brandi Chastain
Abby Wambach
Aly Wagner
Carli Lloyd
Julie Ertz
Tobin Heath
Alex Morgan

A BRIEF TEAM HISTORY

The US women's national team leads all nations with three World Cup titles. The first came in 1991, then in 1999, and most recently in 2015. As World Cups go, the US also has three third-place finishes and a second-place title to its name. From the 1996 Olympics to today, the US women have won an astounding four gold medals and one silver.

Within CONCACAF, what is referred to as the CONCACAF Championship and Gold Cup, the US women have dominated the competition, having won eight championships since 1991. In the Algarve Cup, which was hosted in Portugal, the US women have earned 10 championship titles.

Throughout women's international soccer history, the US women have dominated almost completely. There are a number of factors for their success. Back in the 1970s, when soccer was coming to fruition as a popular youth sport in America, the leagues would sometimes be co-ed, allowing the girls an opportunity to gain experience and expand their skillset and all-around gamesmanship. Another interesting facet to this development was that the soccer programs available for women drastically increased in popularity in the 1980s. Members of the 1999 World Cup team, such as Michelle Akers and Mia Hamm, were part of this slow-moving wave of female soccer in America. And, quite frankly, collegiate sports for women were not widely available in other countries around the world. If they were, they definitely weren't at the level of colleges in the US. (And even in the US, collegiate women's sports were fighting for equal funding, which is another story.) America definitely had a head start over the rest of the world when it came to soccer. One, American girls were playing in co-ed leagues, a concept not fully encouraged back in the day around the world, and, two, the American girls had an opportunity to play in college as young women. Both of these factors are very important pieces to the puzzle as to why America has been so dominant. The second part, the opportunity to play in college, is very important because college competition gave young American women the opportunity to fine-tune their skills at the highest level in America back then (pre WPS or Women's Professional Soccer, NWSL or National Women's Soccer League). This translated to international success thereafter. So therefore, as international soccer for women started to pick up with the World Cup of 1991, the United States was in charge, to say the least.

Another reason for why America has dominated in women's soccer is based purely on observational opinion: They're just better. They have a knack; they understand the game; they play the game well; their skill level is high. There are, of course, reasons why this is. We touched on two of them earlier, that being the availability of co-ed leagues for girls in the 1970s and 80s along with an outlet for competitive soccer at the college level. In addition, in the 1980s, and largely in the 1990s, female soccer in America was on the rise, becoming more and more popular. Therefore, a natural result included the opening of leagues for girls around the country. Girls were playing club soccer more frequently, going to camps, and gaining insight from the veterans of the emerging US women's soccer team, such as Anson Dorrance, a very smart coach of the US women's national team and of the women's team at North Carolina; April Heinrichs, a legendary player and coach; Tony DiCicco, a well-known coach that led the women's team in 1999; along with many others.

Still, in the early years of the women's World Cup, back when in started in 1991, the international competition just wasn't what it is today. Often female sports, and particularly female soccer, just was not encouraged in other countries back then. Around the world, largely speaking, soccer was for the men. Since that time, things have changed a lot, and consequently, female teams from around the world are drastically improving. The field of competition keeps getting better with time. That said, the US women have continued to dominate international soccer. Somehow, they're just better.

Leading into the 2019 Women's World Cup, the US team had a six-month schedule arranged that included training sessions and friendly games. Andrew Das at *The New York Times* pointed out, "In the past, the team was sometimes informed about the dates of training camps and matches as little as six weeks in advance, which complicated everything from planning vacations and birthdays to scheduling surgeries and weddings. But those short windows also posed problems for the federation, which had less time to sell tickets for the matches; for fans, who might want to travel to them; and for sponsors interested in rolling out marketing plans related to the team."[2]

It was an exciting time for the US women's team. On December 6, 2018, Steven Goff of *The Washington Post* wrote, "The U.S. women's national soccer team will prepare to defend its world title by playing two friendlies in Europe and eight matches at U.S. venues, culminating with a visit to the New York area. In a long-term schedule released by the U.S. Soccer Federation on Thursday, the top-ranked Americans will face five of the top eight teams in the FIFA rankings, including Japan, its opponent in the past two Women's World Cup championship games."[3]

To reiterate, the US women have led world soccer from almost the very beginning. The US women's program has always been the standard by which every other competitor tries to live up to. On its journey to greatness, the US women's team has had a long and interesting World Cup history. Let's take a closer look.

During the 1991 Women's World Cup, which took place in China, the USWNT started out in Group B, a tough group that included Sweden, Brazil, and Japan. The USWNT won its opening game by defeating Sweden 3-2, with goals from Carin Jennings-Gabarra and Mia Hamm. In its second game, the USWNT walked all over Brazil, winning 5-0. At this point, things were looking good for the US. In its last group game, the US took it to Japan with a 3-0 victory. Smooth sailing so far; the US went into the quarterfinals with ease where it would continue to dominate. On route to the semi-finals, the US clobbered Chinese Taipei 7-0. Then, in the semi-finals, the US met Germany and delivered a firm 5-2 defeat. It was set; the final match would be the US against Norway.

Norway had first defeated Italy in the quarterfinals, and then took down Sweden in the semis to arrive in the championship game. The USWNT delivered yet again by defeating Norway 2-1, with both goals coming from Michelle Akers, to earn its first World Cup title.

During the 1995 Women's World Cup, which was hosted by Sweden, the USWNT had an opportunity to repeat as champions. Though, it was evident that such a task would be tricky at best. The US shared Group C with China, Denmark, and Australia. In its first game, the US tied China 3-3. Then came Denmark, but the US walked away with a 2-0 victory, with goals from Tiffeny

Milbrett and the always dependable Kristine Lilly. For its final group game, the US defeated Australia 4-1.

The US advanced to the quarterfinals where it met Japan. The Japanese took a 4-0 defeat. Things were looking good for the US women. However, in the semi-finals, with a chance to move ahead and defend the title from 1991, the US lost a tough game to Norway by 1-0. The team the US had defeated four years earlier in the championship moved ahead and eventually won the tournament, overtaking Germany in the final game. As for the US, it took third after defeating China 2-0 in the consolation game. It was the final game of the tournament for the US. And in four years time it would meet China again, under different circumstances, on home turf.

The famous 1999 Women's World Cup took place in the United States. Host cities included Foxborough, Massachusetts; East Rutherford, New Jersey; Landover, Maryland; Chicago, Illinois; Portland, Oregon; and San Francisco (Stanford), San Jose, and Pasadena, California.

The game was on. The USWNT had a date with destiny—the championship game at the Rose Bowl in Pasadena, California. But first, the US had to get through Group A, which consisted of Nigeria, North Korea, and Denmark. In its opening game, the US defeated Denmark 3-0, with goals from Mia Hamm, Julie Foudy, and Kristine Lilly. Next up, the US walked past Nigeria, 7-1. Lastly, the US was victorious over North Korea, 3-0. In the quarterfinals, the US played Germany and escaped with a 3-2 victory. From there, the US would meet Brazil in the semi-finals. With the weight of a nation eager to see the US in the championship, a 2-0 US victory was the outcome in Stanford

Stadium in front of over 70,000 people. The crowd was in a frenzy, which was nothing compared to what was next.

For the championship game, the USWNT would take on China, a very talented team. On its way to the final, China defeated Russia in the quarterfinals and then stepped past Norway rather easily in the semi-finals. A true showdown was about to take place at the Rose Bowl. It seemed like everyone showed up for this game, and as the teams walked out to the field, chills had to have been rushing through every person in the stadium. With a little over 90,000 people in attendance it was a monumental moment for that particular World Cup, for women's soccer, and for sports history in general. Something was brewing that day and both teams didn't disappoint.

It was a great game, with both sides showing top-level skill, organization, passing, and a will to win. The US wasn't going to walk away with an easy win, that's for sure; China's passing game was very well orchestrated. In fact, what made this game so great was that China was a phenomenal team. Despite the game ending in a 0-0 draw, it was one that felt like the score didn't matter; maybe because the stakes were so high, each moment in the flow of play felt important.

The game went to penalty kicks. Each US player—Overbeck, Fawcett, Lilly, and Hamm—scored their penalty, and with only one Chinese player having missed her shot, it came down to Brandi Chastain to win the World Cup—that's right, to *win the World Cup*—with one kick. Anyone who watched can probably remember that tensions couldn't have been higher. Penalty kicks are seen, by some, as a bad way to end a game. Yet, there are others that believe shootouts provide amazing, indescribable drama. Those who believe in the latter dream of moments like the one Chastain had. In the stands, over 90,000 fans, the equivalent of a large city, were captivated. Then, Chastain approached, and history was made. As she scored there seemed to be a simultaneous eruption from the crowd. Absolute euphoria. Chastain took her shirt off revealing only a sports bra, a picture shown around the world that embodied the spirit of the moment, and the team went wild with celebration.

Without question, hands down, it was a very special moment for women's soccer, soccer in America, female sports, and sports in general. This win established the US as the best team in the world. It was also the second World Cup title for the women's program, which put the US out in front of all competitors.

When World Cup 2003 came around, the USWNT had a chance to defend its title yet again. Coincidently, the tournament was hosted again in the US. Games were held in Foxborough, Massachusetts; Philadelphia, Pennsylvania; Washington D.C.; Columbus, Ohio; Portland, Oregon; and Carson, California.

The US began play in Group A, along with Sweden, North Korea, and Nigeria. The US women kicked things off with a 3-1 win over Sweden. Next up was Nigeria, who the US handled with ease, winning 5-0. Lastly, the US took down North Korea 3-0. Things were looking up, and the US appeared to be on its way back to the championship podium. During the quarterfinals, the US continued its winning streak by beating the talented Norwegians 1-0. However, championship lane was not to be the final destination as the US lost in a disappointing semi-final to Germany by 3-0. Germany went on to win the whole tournament. The United States eventually placed third by defeating Canada in the consolation match.

The 2007 World Cup hosted by China was yet another chance for the US to get back on top. Placed in Group B, the US had to get through North Korea, Sweden, and Nigeria (a little déjà vu). During its first game, the US didn't exactly get the result it wanted with a 2-2 tie against North Korea. Next, the US took on Sweden and got a better result with a 2-0 win. Lastly, to finish up group play, the US defeated Nigeria 1-0. As a result, the US finished at the top of its group, with North Korea in second. During the quarterfinals, the US encountered England but moved on with a 3-0 victory. Things didn't end up as planned in the semi-finals as the US lost big to Brazil by a score of 4-0. Germany went on to win this tournament, and the US placed third overall.

As the 2011 World Cup came around, the US was ready to seize a chance at greatness again. The team hadn't won the World Cup since 1999, and this was a great opportunity to get back in front and reclaim the highest honor in the world. Fabulous Germany hosted, and the games were played in Berlin, Frankfurt, Bochum, Monchengladbach, Sinsheim, Leverkusen, Wolfsburg, Dresden, and Augsburg.

Initially, in Group C, things were looking fairly good for the US. For its first game, the US defeated North Korea 2-0. Then it took down Colombia by a score of 3-0. And finally, the US women took a 2-1 defeat from Sweden. Finishing second in its group allowed the US to move on. As for the quarterfinals, the US was paired against a tough opponent in Brazil but managed to get by. In the semi-finals, the US maneuvered past France by winning 3-1. At this point, the US was back in the championship game and very eager to grab a third title. However, Japan would prove to be a worthy opponent. On route to the final, Japan first defeated Germany in the quarterfinals, and then went by the talented

Swedes in the semis. The final was a good game that tied 2-2 and went to penalties. However, things didn't go so well for the US in the shootout, and Japan took its first World Cup title. Hope Solo was awarded "Best Goalkeeper" of the tournament.

A second-place finish wasn't the worst, but the US women had created a standard of excellence, and anything short of a World Cup championship wasn't good enough. At this point, however, it seemed like the US women were seeking what was becoming an elusive trophy. Would the US win the World Cup again? Was the title of "World Cup champion" becoming a forgotten dream? It had now been over 10 years since the last triumphant World Cup title, and some were beginning to think that the US wasn't as dominant as it once had been.

World Cup 2015 would turn out to be an interesting story altogether. Canada hosted the illustrious tournament. The USWNT had a good team, one that featured Alex Morgan and Carli Lloyd. Starting out in Group D, the US was up against Australia, Sweden, and Nigeria. In its opening game, the US defeated Australia 3-1. In the following game, the US tied the talented Swedes 0-0. Then, as luck would have it, the US got past Nigeria with a 1-0 win. The round of 16 was the next stop, and the USWNT had a date with Colombia that ended up being a 2-0 victory. Following that were the quarterfinals in Ottawa during which the US outscored China by 1-0.

By this point in the tournament, the USWNT was getting into a groove. The team was playing well, but the US would have to prove itself in the semi-finals against a talented German side. A 2-0 score was the result, and the US found itself back in the final, with a great chance at being the first women's team in history to reach three World Cup titles.

The last team they would contend with was Japan, a rematch from 2011. Carli Lloyd had a great game, scoring an amazing hat-trick, and the USWNT did in fact make history by winning the game 5-2 and claiming a third title in the process. As the first team to reach three titles, the USWNT program was in unchartered territory.

Carli Lloyd won the Golden Ball along with the Silver Boot. Hope Solo won the Golden Glove. Also, members of the All-Star team included Hope Solo, Carli Lloyd, Julie Johnston (Julie Ertz), Meghan Klingenberg, and Megan Rapinoe. As the world's best soccer program, it proved once again that it belonged in the number one position.

Now the US has a great opportunity to win its fourth title in France 2019. Entering the tournament, the US was ranked number one in the world, and the team will hope to keep it that way.

FACTS ABOUT THEIR COUNTRY

The USWNT leads all nations with three World Cup titles. Professional women's soccer in the US is currently the National Women's Soccer League (NWSL). It was founded in 2012 and consists of the following teams: Chicago Red Stars (Bridgeview, Illinois), Houston Dash (Houston, Texas), North Carolina Courage (Cary, North Carolina), Orlando Pride (Orlando, Florida), Portland Thorns FC (Portland, Oregon), Seattle Reign FC (Seattle, Washington), Sky Blue FC (Piscataway, New Jersey), Utah Royals FC (Sandy, Utah), and Washington Spirit (Germantown, Maryland).

JILL ELLIS—A BRIEF COACHING PORTRAIT

Jill Ellis, born in England, guided the US women in 2015 to a World Cup championship and is back for another run. With a consecutive title, she would be the first US women's coach to do so. In the past, Ellis has coached with a few universities, including NC State, Maryland, Virginia, Illinois, and UCLA. She's leading a super-talented team in France, one that FIFA has ranked at number one. With a lot of expectations looming, Ellis should have enough confidence, wisdom, and experience from the previous World Cup to guide the team, at the very least, to the semi-finals. With that said, many people are expecting Ellis to be holding the championship trophy once again.

KEY PLAYERS AND THEIR CHARACTERISTICS

Tobin Heath, Alex Morgan, and Julie Ertz

Tobin Heath is one of a kind, a brilliant dribbler, playmaker, technician on the ball, and all-out threat around goal. Given her skillset and ability to break down defenses, she'll definitely go down as one of America's greatest. With that said, she might also go down as a player with "Denilson syndrome," referring, of course, to Denilson of Brazil on the men's side…a player who, arguably, was the most impactful member on Brazil, yet he came off the bench. Whether Heath comes off the bench or not, or does not make the World Cup All-Star team (as was the case in 2015), is yet to be seen. Another axiom in Heath's situation is that America has too many good players, so the coach is pressed to play as many people as possible. Regardless, at any given time, Heath will be the most impactful player on the field. And, from time to time, gifted offensive players like her, for one reason or another, might not make an All-Star team.

Alex Morgan is a gifted attacking player with an eye for the goal. She struggled with overcoming an injury in the 2015 World Cup but managed to play well and was an integral part of that championship run. In France, Morgan is looking to add another World Cup title to her résumé. With Morgan playing well, the US is undoubtedly a number one team to contend with.

Julie Ertz, who is originally from Arizona, brings playing experience from Santa Clara University and Chicago Red Stars. She's full of talent, and, leading into the 2019 World Cup, FIFA had listed her as the star player for the US team. In France, she'll be guiding the team from midfield with an assortment of talent at her disposal. Many people are expecting Julie and the team to exit France with first-place medals. En route to that goal, Ertz has the pressure of bringing everything together. If she can assert herself on the field, and find the right rhythm of passing with the brilliant US defenders, then things should be clicking on all cylinders with Megan Rapinoe, Alex Morgan, and others. That is essentially the task at hand for Ertz: to orchestrate everything and find the right balance. She's definitely up to the task.

KEY PLAYER STATS
(Total career goals with their country)

	Games Played	Goals
Tobin Heath	143	25
Alex Morgan	155	98
Julie Ertz	74	18

WHAT TO WATCH FOR ON TV—HOW MARTA, MORGAN, HEATH, AND OTHERS PLAY

The combination up top of Tobin Heath, Alex Morgan, and Julie Ertz alone should be enough to keep opponents off-balance. Add to the equation players like Kelley O'Hara, Crystal Dunn, Megan Rapinoe, Lindsey Horan, and Rose Lavelle, and you have a total package that is likely going to win the whole thing. This is a team that is expected to repeat as champs. As the FIFA world number one, the biggest story might be if the US loses and how it loses. But for all intents and purposes, watch for the US winning, and winning big. US teams traditionally are technically sound, creative, good dribblers, smart, intuitive, organized, very strong on one-on-one defense, formidable on group defense, accurate passers, and good finishers. This squad of 2019 is no different.

Tactics and strategies: While the US is clearly the favorite, there a few things it has to its advantage. First of all, advanced passing comes to mind when watching the US play. It's a team that can dazzle and keep opponents off-balance with superior touch on the ball, combination passing, and elaborate through-balls into space. Should the USWNT follow a strict approach to possession for possession's sake, it could completely take away the game plan from any opponent. However, what will likely be the case is that the US will go at teams using possession with purpose. (For those unfamiliar with the practice of *possession with purpose*, it is getting to the scoring part of the game without long stints of possession for possession's sake). The US has the talent to really go after opponents using possession with purpose, and it will very likely—in fact, more than likely—take this approach. When a team like the US has such superior talent, it's hard not to. Expect to see a lot of free-flowing soccer, like that of Brazil in 1970, with an extra twist of organization.

When Carli Lloyd, Alex Morgan, Tobin Heath, and Julie Ertz are on your team, good things are going to happen. The only thing that might hold the team back would be the pressure. Aside from that, if the US can play normal soccer, soccer without a conscience, it should make a very good run at the title.

Overall Team Ranking: 9.9
FIFA Ranking Going Into the World Cup: 1

FRANCE

Twitter @FIFAWWC*
World Cup titles: 0
European Championships: 0

Known for:
Hosting the 2019 Women's World Cup
Exciting games
Corinne Diacre
Amandine Henry
Valerie Gauvin

A BRIEF TEAM HISTORY

From 1991 to 1999, France did not qualify for the Women's World Cup. Then, in 2003, France qualified and competed in the United States but didn't get out of its group. France didn't qualify in 2007; though in 2011 it made the World Cup and eventually placed fourth overall. Not bad. As for World Cup 2015, in

---

* A Twitter account for the women's national team of France could not be found. Instead, FIFA's Twitter account could possibly guide you to information about France's team.

familiar Canadian territory, France made it to the round of 16 where it defeated South Korea. Then, in the quarterfinals, France was eliminated by the talented Germans. Currently, in 2019, France is the host with an eye on doing very well in front of a supportive home crowd. France entered the tournament ranked third in the world by FIFA.

FACTS ABOUT THEIR COUNTRY

The 2019 World Cup is the first women's World Cup France has hosted. France is known for great art, food, and wine. For wine tasting, tourists and World Cup fans alike might want to try Domaine Charles Joguet, Chateau Feely, Castle Cremat, Chateau de Pommard, or Gitton Pere & Fils.

CORINNE DIACRE—A BRIEF COACHING PORTRAIT

Corinne Diacre, born in France, played as a defender with ASJ Soyaux; she also played with the French national team from 1993 to 2005. Diacre is guiding the third ranked team in the world with home-field advantage to boot. With the added pressure of winning at home, should France win the whole thing, Diacre would make history as the first women's coach to do so in her country.

KEY PLAYERS AND THEIR CHARACTERISTICS

Amandine Henry and Valerie Gauvin

Amandine Henry is a talented played who has experience with a number of teams, including Paris Saint-Germain Feminines and Olympique Lyonnais Feminin. Keep an eye on her in the midfield for offensive and defensive responsibilities.

Valerie Gauvin, who is originally from Reunion Island, is a forward who has experience with Toulouse FC and Montpellier.

KEY PLAYER STATS
(Total career goals with their country)

	Games Played	Goals
Amandine Henry	74	11
Valerie Gauvin	10	5

WHAT TO WATCH FOR ON TV—HOW MARTA, MORGAN, HEATH, AND OTHERS PLAY

Possibly operating out of a 4-4-2 or perhaps a 4-2-3-1, at defense you have Marion Torrent, Aissatou Tounkara, Amel Majri; in the midfield you'll find Viviane Asseyi, Grace Geyoro, Amandine Henry, Eugenie Le Sommer; and at forward will be Gaetane Thiney and Valerie Gauvin. Along with other talented players at its disposal, France, the world number three going into the 2019 World Cup, is a strong team and one of the favorites this time around.

Tactics and strategies: One thing France must take into consideration and pay very close attention to will be its defensive backline and how well the defensive backline can distribute the ball. This will be key. If the defenders can affectively distribute the ball in an organized fashion, and with deft touch, then good things will result over the span of the tournament. But, and this is very important, if France loses focus of this strategy, or let's call it, approach, then bad things will start to unfold in terms of giveaways, which may result in an onslaught of shots on its goal. That's not where France wants to be. The approach France wants to take has everything to do with defenders passing the ball artistically, wisely, and with deft touch. This will define France on the field. It wants to control the flow of play; it wants to dominate the passing end of the game; and this starts with the defenders. After all, in any given soccer game, it's the defenders who, most often, have the majority of touches on the ball. It's not the midfielders or forwards, it's the defenders. (Go figure! Amazing, right?) This is why defenders are so crucial to the flow of play when it comes to distributing the ball. The ball has to be distributed with smart ideas, rhythm, and artistic touch. If France can control these things and excel at these things, then it will be in good shape. But again, to reiterate, it's going to start with the French defenders. Watch for them. See if they have control of the game in this regard. The French midfielders and forwards will be depending on them. Furthermore, home-field advantage will play a huge role in France's success.

With the majority of its players enlisted with French clubs, France will definitely have a domestic style to its approach, one that should involve fluid passing and a swift buildup in the attack.

Overall Team Ranking: 9.5
FIFA Ranking Going Into the World Cup: 3

SOUTH KOREA

Twitter @FIFAWWC*
World Cup titles: 0
AFC Women's Asian Cup: 0

Known for:
Ji So-yun
Jeon Ga-eul
Jung Seol-bin
Cho So-hyun

A BRIEF TEAM HISTORY

From 1991 to 1999, South Korea did not qualify for the Women's World Cup. In 2003, the South Koreans qualified for the World Cup but finished last in Group B. Then, the South Koreans failed to qualify for the World Cups of 2007 and 2011. However, in 2015, South Korea was back in the World Cup and had its best showing to date. In Group E, competing with Brazil, Costa Rica,

---

* A Twitter account for the women's national team of South Korea could not be found. Instead, FIFA's Twitter account could possibly guide you to information about South Korea's team.

and Spain, the South Koreans finished second behind Brazil and qualified for the elimination rounds. Though, South Korea's luck would run out in the round of 16 where it lost to France. South Korea won the 2005 EAFF Women's Football Championship. (EAFF stands for East Asian Football Federation.)

FACTS ABOUT THEIR COUNTRY

Seoul is the capitol of South Korea, and the nation's population is approximately 51 million people. Interesting beers that might be making the rounds as fans watch the World Cup on TV include Hite, Max, and OB (Oriental Brewery). Some nights when ordering takeout, Korean food is the perfect option. Luckily, for South Koreans, every night is an option for great food. While beers are being passed around, South Koreans also have the luxury of a very unique cuisine which may feature Kimchi (vegetables), Bulgogi (a version of beef barbeque), along with Japchae (tasty noodles which are stir-fried).

YOON DEOK-YEO—A BRIEF COACHING POR-TRAIT

Yoon Deok-yeo was a defender with the men's South Korean national team. He also brings to the table playing experience with Pohang Steelers, Ulsan Hyundai FC, and Hanil Bank FC. As a former defender, Yoon Deok-yeo will concentrate on strong defense in France 2019, which entails team organization and good defensive shape. This should be evident in South Korea's first group match, and, if done correctly, South Korea's offense should develop nicely as a result.

KEY PLAYERS AND THEIR CHARACTERISTICS

Ji So-yun, Jeon Ga-eul, Jung Seol-bin, and Cho So-hyun

Ji So-yun, born in 1991 in South Korea, has over 100 caps with her national team. She's a midfielder who also has experience with INAC Kobe Leonessa and Chelsea.

Jeon Ga-eul, born in 1988, will be found up front in the attack. Since 2007, she's done well for South Korea, scoring over 35 goals.

Jung Seol-bin, born in 1990, is a forward with over 70 appearances for South Korea.

Cho So-hyun has a lot of experience with South Korea, playing in over 100 games thus far in her career. She recently has joined West Ham United Women in England. She's a midfielder who will add valuable experience and organization for South Korea's chances to move forward in the tournament.

KEY PLAYER STATS
(Total career goals with their country)

	Games Played	Goals
Ji So-yun	109	49
Jeon Ga-eul	96	38
Jung Seol-bin	72	20
Cho So-hyun	115	20

WHAT TO WATCH FOR ON TV—HOW MARTA, MORGAN, HEATH, AND OTHERS PLAY

Ji So-Yun, Jeon Ga-eul, Jung Seol-bin, Lee Eun-mi, Lim Seon-joo, Cho So-hyun, Lee So-dam, Lee Geum-min, and Kim Hye-ri, among others, present a formidable test for any opponent. FIFA had South Korea ranked at 14 going into the tournament, but still it's a team that has the players, experience, and expertise to go far in this tournament. Expect a high work rate and effort from the South Koreans, a group eager to have a huge World Cup.

Tactics and strategies: Possession soccer should be a key for South Korea. That is to say, if South Korea can combine this with strategic counterattacks, then it should be in decent shape. Though, it seems unlikely that South Korea will blow teams away with outright speed on the wings. It's a team that will find success with a patient buildup in possession and by utilizing a swift counter when appropriate. Finding a balance between these two things will be very important if South Korea plans on getting into the elimination rounds. Though, South Korea should put more of its focus on possession for possession's sake, and scoring opportunities will present themselves more frequently.

If keeping up with one's neighbor is an important motivational force, then look no further than South Korea who has seen Japan in the World Cup finals for the past two tournaments. Talk about inspiration. Indeed, South Korea has the potential to make a big push this tournament. It's a group that can equal what Japan has done in recent years. Who knows, this might be the year South Korea breaks through and into the final match.

Overall Team Ranking: 8.6
FIFA Ranking Going Into the World Cup: 14

NORWAY

Twitter @FIFAWWC*
World Cup titles: 1
European Championships: 2

Known for:
Winning the World Cup in 1995
Very passionate fans
Quality performances
Maren Mjelde
Emilie Haavi
Lisa-Marie Karlseng Utland

A BRIEF TEAM HISTORY

Norway has been a strong presence in past World Cups. In 1991, the Norwegians placed second. Then, picking up where it left off, Norway walked away with the championship in 1995. In 1999, during the epic World Cup held in the United States,

---

* A Twitter account for the women's national team of Norway could not be found. Instead, FIFA's Twitter account could possibly guide you to information about Norway's team.

Norway placed a respectable fourth. The next time around, during the 2003 World Cup, Norway lost in the quarterfinals to the US. During the 2007 World Cup in China, Norway had a better showing, earning fourth place. As for World Cup 2011, Norway didn't fair too well. In Group D with Brazil, Australia, and Equatorial Guinea, Norway failed to advance to the elimination rounds. Most recently, during the 2015 World Cup held in Canada, Norway lost in the round of 16 to England.

Norway won the gold medal at the 2000 Olympics, along with two European Women's Championships (the European Competition for Women's Football and the UEFA Women's Euro) and four first-place finishes at the Algarve Cup.

FACTS ABOUT THEIR COUNTRY

Norway is a Scandinavian country with a population of around 5 million people. A few beers the citizens of Norway might be enjoying during the World Cup include Hansa, Arendals, Ringnes, Borg, and Grans. Norway is known for fjords, a beautiful natural wonder. Thesse fjords are long, narrow inlets with steep cliffs which have been created by a glacier. In some cases, fjords will be a backdrop as fans watch the games on TV.

MARTIN SJOGREN—A BRIEF COACHING PORTRAIT

Martin Sjogren, born in 1977, began coaching Norway in 2016, and his goal this World Cup is to add a second cup to Norway's trophy case. Sjogren attended the University of North Florida in the past, and he might just be the coach to deliver an upset to the USWNT this year.

KEY PLAYERS AND THEIR CHARACTERISTICS

Maren Mjelde, Emilie Haavi, and Lisa-Marie Karlseng Utland

Maren Mjelde, born in 1989 in Norway, was listed by FIFA as Norway's top player leading into the 2019 World Cup. She's got a ton of experience with her national team, playing in over 130 games so far in her illustrious career. She's currently playing with Chelsea, and this experience should serve her well on a quest to win the World Cup in France. With her leadership and organizational capability, Norway, a team that is usually a tough competitor, should have a good tournament.

Emilie Haavi, born in 1992, is a forward with experience most recently at LSK Kvinner FK in Norway. Since 2010, she's played with her national team, gaining over 70 caps, with plenty of years to go in her career. In this World Cup, she'll look to capitalize on opportunities in the box while also keeping a good eye out for assisting teammates.

Lisa-Marie Karlseng Utland, born in 1992, is a forward with quite a bit of youth national team experience and someone to watch this tournament. She will likely be a player who might have an important role with the team on its quest to gaining a World Cup title.

KEY PLAYER STATS

(Total career goals with their country)

	Games Played	Goals
Maren Mjelde	132	19
Emilie Haavi	76	15
Lisa-Marie Karlseng Utland	35	10

WHAT TO WATCH FOR ON TV—HOW MARTA, MORGAN, HEATH, AND OTHERS PLAY

Maren Mjelde, Emilie Haavi, Caroline Graham Hansen, Lisa-Marie Karlseng Utland, Guro Reiten, Kristine Minde, and Isabell Herlovsen are a few of the talented players that make up a strong Norwegian side ready to make a major splash this World Cup.

Tactics and strategies: Norwegian teams of yore would have you think that chucking up long-balls down the field was the only way to approach a game. While times—and team strategy—may have changed a bit, you can still expect to see some long-ball tactics from Norway, but with more of a cultured touch. Expect to see crosses into the box, with Norway getting numbers up and into the attack, looking to capitalize on all opportunities possible. In doing so, distribution from the defenders will be very important, as they control the flow of play. Norway needs to have strong and savvy contributions from its midfield in order to create a pulse between players. Lastly, and possibly the most important point for Norway, the forwards need to check back for the ball routinely and make simple passes to give the midfielders and defenders constructive passing outlets.

Abby Wambach, to her credit, did this well. If Norway can steal a page from her book, then it'll be in good shape. What Wambach did so well was checking back into space, essentially coming back into the midfield area, and then playing the ball right back to the player that passed to her or someone nearby. (By and large, this creates a good avenue for the attack to work its way down field.) This establishes a rhythm between players, more players get touches on the ball, chemistry forms, and a vital link between the forwards and midfielders is formed, and, not to mention, this link includes defenders as well. It's so important for forwards to check back and play with their back to goal such as this, because, again, it brings the midfielders and defenders together, and, if done correctly, everything is flowing like a brand new car engine.

The opposite of this tactic is to post a forward up next to the last defender and never check back for the ball. The idea here is to have a forward as close to the goal as possible as a target player for crosses and long-balls. A downside to this approach is that passing lanes tend to dry up, and, as a result, chemistry between players can suffer. Typically this is not a good idea. Norway should avoid doing this as much as possible.

The last—and only—World Cup title Norway has dates back to its glorious year of 1995. It's a team and country ready to embrace that experience again. So expect to see a very determined Norwegian side, with a strong work rate and good team unity. Anything less would be a recipe for disaster. Norway is certainly aware of this and it should bring its A game every outing.

Overall Team Ranking: 8.7
FIFA Ranking Going Into the World Cup: 13

NIGERIA

Twitter @thenff @NGSuper_Falcons
World Cup titles: 0
Africa Women's Championships: 11

Known for:
Past World Cup appearances
Underdog team
Francisca Ordega
Asisat Oshoala

A BRIEF TEAM HISTORY

As far as World Cups go, Nigeria has qualified for each one since 1991; however, it hasn't gotten out of the group stage except for one time in 1999 when it reached the quarterfinals where it was defeated by Brazil. Aside from World Cup challenges, Nigeria has done well in the Africa Women's Championship (the CAF Africa Cup of Nations for Women), winning it 11 times.

FACTS ABOUT THEIR COUNTRY

Located on the west coast of Africa, Nigeria is approximately the size of Texas and has a population of around 198 million people. Its capital city is Abuja, and there are a number of languages spoken in Nigeria, a few of which include English, Hausa, Igbo, and Yoruba. Soccer is the most popular sport in Nigeria, and the women's national team has qualified for every World Cup since 1991.

THOMAS DENNERBY—A BRIEF COACHING PORTRAIT

Thomas Dennerby, born in 1959 in Sweden, began coaching the Nigerian women's side in 2018, and to say he's leading an underdog would be an understatement. Going into the World Cup, FIFA had Nigeria ranked at 39 worldwide. Essentially, Dennerby and Nigeria have a challenging road ahead just to get into the elimination rounds.

KEY PLAYERS AND THEIR CHARACTERISTICS

Francisca Ordega and Asisat Oshoala

Francisca Ordega, born in 1993, is a forward with her eyes on World Cup greatness. She has experience with a number of clubs, including Washington Spirit in the US.

Asisat Oshoala, born in 1994, is a forward who has played with Dalian Quanjian F.C., Arsenal W.F.C., and Liverpool F.C.

Women, to name a few. Leading into the 2019 World Cup, FIFA had listed Oshoala as Nigeria's top player.

KEY PLAYER STATS

(Total career goals with their country)

	Games Played	Goals
Francisca Ordega	7	26
Asisat Oshoala	17	11

WHAT TO WATCH FOR ON TV—HOW MARTA, MORGAN, HEATH, AND OTHERS PLAY

Francisca Ordega and Asisat Oshoala are part of a Nigerian effort that is facing a tough challenge. If Nigeria is going to get into the elimination rounds, it will require a lot of hard work, a strong game plan, and a lot of luck.

Tactics and strategies: Nigeria should concentrate on a fluid counterattack as its best offensive weapon. And indeed it probably will. As an underdog, oftentimes a swift counter is all you've got. Count on Nigeria to swarm its opponent with defense, followed by quick counters into space. The key here will be on Nigeria delivering accurate passes into space, thus affording it an opportunity to catch opponents off guard. It's a tricky strategy because by using it you're essentially eliminating possession as a means to control a game. Possession, and a lot of it, would be a better approach. However, let's face it, leading into this World Cup, Nigeria was ranked number 39 in the world. Usually (not always, but usually) teams of this ranking are not masters at passing combinations and possession-oriented soccer. Therefore, Nigeria must concentrate on strong defense and multiple counterattacks for any chance of success.

It's a team with multiple World Cup runs in the past that have not delivered results. With a low world ranking, it would be asking a lot for Nigeria to win this World Cup or even get into the quarterfinals. If you gamble, place your money elsewhere. However, with that said, it should be interesting to see just how well Nigeria can do this time around.

Overall Team Ranking: 6.1
FIFA Ranking Going Into the World Cup: 39

GERMANY

Twitter @DFB_Team_EN*
World Cup titles: 2
European Championships: 8

Known for:
Two World Cup titles
High-quality teams
A well-established program
Exciting games
Heidi Mohr
Bettina Wiegmann
Birgit Prinz
Inka Grings
Dzsenifer Marozsan
Alexandra Popp
Sara Dabritz

---

*   No other Twitter account was found for the German women's soccer
team.

A BRIEF TEAM HISTORY

At the 1991 World Cup, Germany started out in Group C with Italy, Chinese Taipei, and Nigeria. In its first game against Nigeria, Germany won 4-0. In the following game, Germany had a good result against Chinese Taipei, winning 3-0. Lastly, against Italy, Germany won 2-0, thus finishing at the top of the group, with Italy in second, and Chinese Taipei in third. During the quarterfinals, Germany met Denmark, its European neighbor to the north, and won 2-1. Germany's success came to a screeching halt in the semi-finals against the mighty US, whereby it lost 5-2. Eventually, the Germans placed fourth overall, after losing in the consolation match to Sweden 4-0. Despite the fourth-place finish, it was a good opening World Cup for Germany, and a sign of good things to come.

At the 1995 World Cup held in Sweden, Germany began in Group A alongside Sweden, Japan, and Brazil. A tough group to say the least. But the Germans were ready for the task at hand. In its first game against Japan, the Germans snuck away with a 1-0 win. In the next challenge, Germany took a 3-2 loss against Sweden. Then, as if to make up for it, Germany took it to Brazil with an astounding 6-1 victory. Despite the loss to Sweden, Germany won the group, with Sweden in second and Japan in third. During the quarterfinals, Germany defeated its rival England 3-0. Following that were the semi-finals against China during which the Germans managed to win 1-0. The final wouldn't be so kind to Germany as it lost to the talented Norwegians 2-0. A second-place finish. It was an improvement from the previous World Cup, but still not the grand prize.

At the 1999 World Cup, Germany shared Group B with Brazil, Italy, and Mexico. In its opening game, Germany reached a 1-1 tie with Italy. Not the best result, but at least it wasn't a loss. In game number two, things were different for the German team. Mexico was the recipient of a lopsided 6-0 German scoring frenzy. Germany was on a roll. Next up was Brazil, and the Germans got a 3-3 tie. As things in group play finished up, the Germans finished second behind Brazil and managed to move on to the quarterfinals. This wasn't the World Cup for Germany. In the quarterfinals against hosts, the United States, who would go on to win the whole thing, Germany lost 3-2.

So far, the Germans have had a pretty good World Cup experience, placing fourth in 1991, second in 1995, and experiencing a 1999 quarterfinal defeat. The latter would be the most disappointing, obviously. Though, at the same time, one could have viewed it as a learning experience. Germany had to step back, reanalyze, and get ready for the next World Cup in 2003. The Germans had a lot to build on, and good things were around the corner.

In 2003, the Germans were back in the US, where the World Cup was hosted yet again. Possibly this time around, with some previous experience on US soil, the Germans would be better prepared. Would Germany have better luck? Would it prevail? Placed in Group C, the Germans were up against Canada, Japan, and Argentina. Right off the bat, the Germans had a great result against Canada, winning 4-1 in Columbus, Ohio. Next up was Japan, a game which the Germans won 3-0. Finally, against Argentina, Germany had its easiest game of the group, winning 6-1. With these three group wins, Germany won its group and moved on to the quarterfinals.

Waiting for the Germans in the quarterfinals was Russia. But the Russians were no match for the amazing Germans. The game ended in a 7-1 victory for Germany, and it moved on to the next round in which the Germans couldn't have had a tougher challenge in the semi-finals. It was Germany against the United States, the hosts *and* defending champs. The game was played in Portland, Oregon, an enthusiastic soccer city, in front of over 27,000 people. The US had plans of holding on to the belt and repeating as champions. Germany, however, had other ideas and delivered a resounding 3-0 defeat to the United States on home soil. There was no looking back for Germany as it went into the championship game held in Carson, California. Over 26,000 were in attendance to see Germany against a talented Swedish side. No matter who the victor, there was going to be a new champion. As it turned out, that champion would be Germany, who won 2-1. There had been a lot of work for the Germans coming into this World Cup, along with the struggle it endured in 1999. Though World Cup 2003 was a monumental one for Germany, and it was a team looking for more.

World Cup 2007 was going to be a good one. The four prior World Cups were great, and things were only getting better. The illustrious Germans must have been thinking the same thing as the tournament kicked off in China. Initially, in Group A, the Germans went up against England, Japan, and Argentina. Argentina was going to be an easy win; it was England and Japan that were cause for concern. In its first match, Germany defeated Argentina, though "defeated" is probably the wrong word. In fact, it *is* the wrong word. When the score is 11-0, which it was, the term "devastated" comes to mind, as in Germany completely devastated Argentina by a score of, yes, this is correct, 11-0. (So much for Argentina's hope at a title.) In its second game, Germany had a less exciting 0-0 draw with England. As for its last group match, Germany defeated Japan 2-0. Germany won Group

A, with England in second. Japan came in third, and, as you may have guessed by now, Argentina was last. Both Germany and England moved on.

Germany was rolling forward with great momentum, and it was going to be hard for anyone to stop it. First, in the quarterfinals, the Germans dismantled North Korea 3-0. Following that, in the semi-finals, again, Germany won by a score of 3-0 as it overcame a talented Norwegian side. The grand finale, the World Cup final, which took place in Hongkou Football Stadium (Shanghai, China), was yet another shutout for Germany as it beat Brazil 2-0. In doing so, Germany made history as the first women's team to win two consecutive World Cups in a row. It was a remarkable achievement for the Germans. At that time, only Germany and the United States had two World Cup titles.

When the 2011 World Cup in Germany came around, the Germans had a unique opportunity to capture a third title in a row while playing at home. Was there added pressure to host and win three in a row? Probably. But it didn't hurt either. Right out of the gate, Germany found itself navigating through a tricky group. Group A featured Germany, the defending champs, along with France, Nigeria, and Canada. Germany got off to a good start, defeating Canada 2-1. Next, in a game against Nigeria, the Germans got a 1-0 victory. So far, so good. Germany kept up its winning streak against France, grabbing a 4-2 win. In the quarterfinals, Germany's luck came to a sudden halt as it lost 1-0 to Japan, the eventual champions. With that, Germany, a great champion, lost its chance to win three titles in a row.

In the 2015 World Cup, the Germans had something to prove. It had a chance to regain control of world soccer, a great opportunity to win its third title, though not consecutively. After all, three in a row would've been nice, but three total is special no matter how you look at it. Canada was the beautiful setting for this World Cup. And in Group B the Germans were up against Norway, Thailand, and Ivory Coast. From the outset, it was assumed pretty much across the board that Germany wouldn't have much trouble with the less experienced Ivory Coast. And, indeed, such speculation turned out to be true as the Germans walked away with a 10-0 win. Evidently, Ivory Coast approached the game with a 4-2-3-1 formation. Whether that was the case or not, it really didn't matter. The game ended 10-0.

In its next game, Germany went up against a seasoned opponent, Norway. As usual, Norway brought a good team, and the game ended in a 1-1 tie. Lastly, Germany finished off Thailand with a 4-0 victory. With that, Germany won its group, and Norway came in second. In the round of 16, Germany had a tough opponent in the form of Sweden. With a 4-1 victory, Germany moved into the quarterfinals where it defeated France in penalty kicks for a place in the illustrious semi-finals. A great showdown was set between two of the best teams in the world: Germany and the United States. The game took place in Montreal, and on this particular occasion, the United States sent Germany packing as the game ended 2-0. Germany took fourth place after losing the consolation game to England by a score of 1-0.

Unfortunately for Germany, it lost a chance at winning its third World Cup title. Instead, the United States eventually won the tournament and became the first women's team to win three World Cups. With that, the US was back on top of world soccer with three titles, and Germany was in second place with two.

There's always a chance for Germany to gain its third title, which brings us to World Cup 2019. Despite the US being ranked number one in the world going into the tournament, Germany was ranked number two. Will there be a showdown between the two? Most soccer fans would hope so. Along with its many successes, Germany also won the gold medal at the 2016 Olympics. With all this experience behind it, Germany is counting on France 2019 to be spectacular.

FACTS ABOUT THEIR COUNTRY

Germany has a population of around 82 million. It's a great place to vacation with amazing wine, beer, food, and sight-seeing. With so many beers to choose from, Germans watching the games on TV might kick back with a Bavarian-style Weihenstephan Hefe Weissbier, or possibly a well-regarded Paulaner Salvator Doppel Bock. Another delight, quite often found around Cologne, is Gaffel Kolsch. And, of course, there's always Bitburger. Germany isn't just the king of beers. It also produces high-quality automobiles such as BMW and Mercedes. When it comes to soccer, you'll also find that the high-end sporting gear of Adidas and Puma come from Germany as well. In fact, Adidas was started up by two brothers who eventually had a falling out. Nick Carbone, writing for *TIME*, reported, "It's said that the brothers never spoke again, and their bitter rivalry even divided the town of Herzogenaurach, where they built their competing factories on the opposite banks of the town's river. It wasn't until September 2009, long after the brothers' deaths, that the companies put aside their feud and faced off in a friendly game of soccer— an appropriate meeting for two companies who've become independently famous in the field of sports shoes."[4]

MARTINA VOSS-TECKLENBURG—A BRIEF COACHING PORTRAIT

Horst Hrubesch—a former forward with the West German national team and experienced coach—had overseen the German women's national team since the release of Sherri Jones in 2018, just one year before the coveted World Cup in France. As FIFA pointed out, "Germany have parted company with women's national team coach Steffi Jones, the German Football Association (DFB) has announced. Jones was sacked following a disappointing showing at the SheBelieves Cup, in which the team failed to win a single game."[5]

Despite turmoil in the coaching department, Germany managed to be ranked number two in the world as it entered the 2019 World Cup. Regarding the coaching musical chairs, FIFA added, "Martina Voss-Tecklenburg will take over once the France 2019 qualifying campaign finished. During her playing days, Voss-Tecklenburg won six German league titles, four domestic cups and also won the European Championship four times with Germany. She has continued to collect silverware as a coach and in addition to lifting the DFB Cup twice, she also won the UEFA Women's Cup, the precursor to UEFA Women's Champions League. In February 2012 she was appointed Switzerland head coach and guided the team to a maiden qualification for a Women's World Cup."[6] Guiding this team throughout World Cup 2019 will be a formidable task as the squad has to overcome recent hardships, which led to the ousting of Sherri Jones, while also living up to its expectations, which are high.

KEY PLAYERS AND THEIR CHARACTERISTICS

Dzsenifer Marozsan, Alexandra Popp, and Sara Dabritz

Dzsenifer Marozsan was born in 1992 in Hungary and later moved to Germany. Currently, she plays with Olympique Lyonnais Feminin. Germany is relying on Marozsan's ultra-talented midfield skill to guide her team to a third championship in France. Perhaps with her experience playing in Lyon she'll have an added advantage.

Alexandra Popp, born in 1991, is a forward with over 40 goals for Germany in her illustrious career so far. Her experience up top should help Germany get closer to a third championship.

Sara Dabritz was only born in 1995 yet already has veteran status with over 55 caps for Germany.

KEY PLAYER STATS
(Total career goals with their country)

	Games Played	Goals
Dzsenifer Marozsan	86	32
Alexandra Popp	93	44
Sara Dabritz	58	10

WHAT TO WATCH FOR ON TV—HOW MARTA, MORGAN, HEATH, AND OTHERS PLAY

Dzsenifer Marozsan, Alexandra Popp, Sara Dabritz, Sara Doorsoun, Lena Petermann, Lina Magull, Svenja Huth, Babett Peter, Leonie Maier, Carolin Simon, and Kathrin Hendrich are a few of the talented Germans that have helped the team thus far and should play a role in propelling Germany past bewildered opponents this tournament.

Germany, the two-time World Cup champs, is a team anticipating great success in France. Going into this tournament, FIFA had Germany ranked at number two in the world. Many people are expecting a Germany and United States showdown at some point. Be it Brazil, France, Sweden, the United States, or whoever the opposition is, Germany will bring a high level of pressure on defense, with good organization at that, along with a strong passing game that keeps opponents off-balance.

Tactics and strategies: Germany should keep doing what it does best, and that would be team organization and good passing. Germany has a strong defense, that's a given. It needs to focus on keeping the ball away from its opponents and good things will come around in the form of more scoring chances, which usually equals wins.

It's really about Germany using its superior skill over opponents. In doing so, the Germans should also remember to rely on possession for possession's sake. Say what you will about over-possessing the ball, but it works. The odd paradox is that more scoring chances arise. You might ask, how is this possible? Over-possessing the ball literally takes away the will of an opponent.

Over time, throughout the course of a game, this will lead to defensive breakdowns, which is what a team like Germany capitalizes on so well. On the flipside, if over-possession is not used, and, hypothetically speaking, Germany instead relies on trading punches with an opponent, then what happens is both teams are taking shots at one another, giving the opponent a lot of scoring chances. Generally speaking, you don't want that. If you're Germany, you definitely don't want that. A strong defense or not, the less shots Germany has on its goal the better. Over-possession (i.e., possession for possession's sake) takes away the majority of scoring chances an opponent might otherwise get. This is good.

If possible, Germany should rely on its overall prowess in the passing department and remind everyone why it is ranked number two in the world. Whenever Germany is on the field, its players will be of the highest caliber, which makes it a must-see team.

Overall Team Ranking: 9.8
FIFA Ranking Going Into the World Cup: 2

CHINA

Twitter @ChinaWFT
World Cup titles: 0
AFC Women's Asian Cup: 8

Known for:
A strong program
The 1999 World Cup final
Well-played games
Hosting the Women's World Cup twice
Wu Haiyan
Pang Fengyue
Ma Xiaoxu

A BRIEF TEAM HISTORY

China has hosted the World Cup twice, in 1991, the opening tournament, and in 2007. At the 1991 World Cup, China eventually lost out in the quarterfinals. In 1995, at the World Cup in Sweden, China placed fourth. As for the 1999 World Cup, the most famous of them all, China played a huge role in the story as it took second place after losing in a penalty shootout to the United States. During the World Cups of 2003 and 2007, China again lost out in the quarterfinals. For the 2011 World Cup, China, which to this point had a fairly strong World Cup record, didn't qualify. Then, in World Cup 2015, China lost out in the quarterfinals yet again.

China has won the Algarve Cup two times and has won the AFC Women's Championship (also called the AFC Women's Asian Cup) 8 times. As for the Asian Games, China has won it three times, in 1990, 1994, and 1998.

FACTS ABOUT THEIR COUNTRY

While there are 11 players on a field, China has a population of around 1.4 billion people, and, somehow, from the women within the population, it has managed to find a team. While Beijing is China's capitol, which rests in the east, there is expansive land to the west; in the north and northwest you'll find the Gobi Desert.

JIA XIUQUAN—A BRIEF COACHING PORTRAIT

Jia Xiuquan, born in 1963, is a former defender who played for China on the men's national team and ended up coaching a number of teams before taking on the honor of coaching the Chinese women's team. In this World Cup, he is hoping to bring home the championship trophy which the Chinese women's side has gotten close to winning in the past. As always, China has a talented team; though is it safe to assume that China, under Xiuquan's leadership, has a strong challenge ahead? Indeed, that appears to be the case. After all, going into this tournament, FIFA had China ranked at number 15 in the world. While China can certainly handle weaker teams such as Jamaica, a larger concern will be with the higher-ranked sides, such as France, Germany and the US. Having said that, Xiuquan's biggest task might just be to get China past the quarterfinals, which has been an issue for the Chinese over the years.

KEY PLAYERS AND THEIR CHARACTERISTICS

Wu Haiyan, Pang Fengyue, and Ma Xiaoxu

Wu Haiyan, born in 1993, is a defender for the Chinese national team. Since 2012 she's played with China, and with over 65 caps, her country is counting on her experience to help guide the team along.

Pang Fengyue is a midfielder with a lot of experience for China. She also plays with Dalian Quanjian F.C. in China. A key to success might just be how well Fengyue can distribute the ball throughout the tournament.

Ma Xiaoxu is a forward who has played over 150 games for China with a ton of goals on top of that. Watch out for her up top, wheeling and dealing, as China makes a run this tournament.

KEY PLAYER STATS
(Total career goals with their country)

	Games Played	Goals
Wu Haiyan	69	0
Pang Fengyue	87	6
Ma Xiaoxu	152	61

WHAT TO WATCH FOR ON TV—HOW MARTA, MORGAN, HEATH, AND OTHERS PLAY

A few players at China's disposal include Wu Haiyan, Li Ying, Pang Fengyue, Ma Xiaoxu, Liu Shanshan, Wang Shanshan, Zhang Rui, Wang Shuang, Gu Yasha, along with the experienced leadership of Li Dongna.

China has a very strong program, and, regardless who takes the field, expect to see a talented team with organized passing, a strong work rate, a formidable defense, and team unity—a team that is ready to grab the World Cup trophy. An interesting development is going on in the world of tech which has similarities to women's soccer. As Dorothy Wickenden pointed out in a 2019 article from *The New Yorker*, "Silicon Valley may be the center of the tech world right now, but Kai-Fu Lee says that's going to change, and fast. Lee—a computer scientist who worked at Apple, Microsoft, and Google before becoming a venture capitalist—predicts that China will soon overtake the United States as the world leader in innovation."[7]

Generally speaking, for years, China has clearly been a strong player in tech, and, it has been a strong player in women's international soccer. In both fields, it has been keeping up with the US. In terms of women's soccer, China came so close to surpassing the United States at the 1999 World Cup (during the dot-com bubble), but it came in second. Today, after years of ups and downs, China has an amazing opportunity to take France by storm with athletic innovation of its own. While the tech world has ongoing windows of opportunity available for players to introduce a world-changing idea, the window of opportunity at this moment in women's soccer is that of World Cup 2019, and this could be the year that China surpasses the US in women's soccer with innovation, craft, guile, and exquisite technique. It's all right there for China to take. If it can seize this opportunity, for once China can hold the World Cup trophy.

Tactics and strategies: En route to becoming world champion, China must focus on its keys to success, which include team passing, good defensive shape, along with quick counterattacks when possible. China is not going to blow anyone out of the water with someone like Mia Hamm using speed, craft, and guile to dribble around multiple defenders en route to goal. Every once in a while, perhaps, a Chinese player will show off a bit, but expect to see less of this. China's strength rests in its ability to out-pass an opponent. Possession for possession's sake will be a good card for China to hold throughout the tournament. Should it rely on this tactic, good things will follow. Over-possession is a strength to embrace, not to push away. Hopefully, for China's sake, it takes advantage of this. On defense, China needs to stay organized and keep good defensive shape at all times. Any lapses in defense could leave China vulnerable to a goal or two, and at the World Cup level, when all goals matter, the last place it wants to be is down on the scoreboard. Staying focused and keeping good defensive shape will help prevent such a thing from occurring.

Lastly, while China is working away with organized possession-oriented soccer, coupled with a sound defense, it needs to counterattack as often as possible. If China embraces an opportunity to counterattack, this will help balance its overall approach, which, in turn, will keep opponents off balance. Keep in mind, when China attempts a counterattack and turns the ball over, this is fine, and it's something to be expected from any team. Once China turns the ball over it needs to refocus, regroup, think defensively, find its shape, and then pressure the ball away from its opponent. This is easier said than done; however, since China is a possession-oriented team, it can use this in its favor. Typically speaking, possession-oriented teams frustrate opponents by having the ball for long durations of time. In turn, its opponent will turn the ball over quite easily because they are so unaccustomed to having the ball in the first place. In general, China should not get frazzled over low-scoring games. If it sticks to its game plan, and remains focused, it should go far in this World Cup.

Overall Team Ranking: 8.9
FIFA Ranking Going Into the World Cup: 15

SPAIN

Twitter @FIFAWWC*
World Cup titles: 0
European Championships: 0

Known for:
Growing a program
Jorge Vilda
Jennifer Hermoso

A BRIEF TEAM HISTORY

Spain didn't qualify for World Cups 1991 through 2011. As for the 2015 World Cup, history was made as Spain qualified and... didn't get out of its group. But getting to its first World Cup was a big deal. While men's soccer in Spain is flourishing, the women's side is slowly catching up. World Cup 2019, Spain's second, is a great chance to make up for lost time. In fact, with this World Cup record, or lack thereof, it may come as a surprise that FIFA had

---

* A Twitter account for the women's national team of Spain could not be found. Instead, FIFA's Twitter account could possibly guide you to information about Spain's team.

Spain ranked at number 12 in the world leading into France 2019. So this might be the year that Spain makes a big move.

FACTS ABOUT THEIR COUNTRY

Madrid is the capital of Spain and the country has a population of around 46 million. Spain is a dream come true for tourists. Barcelona is one of the leading cities to check out. *The New York Times* recommends a fine hotel experience, as it pointed out, **"Hotel Casa Fuster,** one of Barcelona's classiest hotels, is housed in a 1908-11 Modernista mansion. Check out the romantic Café Vienese and the rooftop terrace and pool with spectacular views."[8] Perhaps when World Cup 2019 finishes up, fans could stop by this location for a jaunt in Spain.

En route to Barcelona from France, one might go through the Basque Country which resides in the north of Spain, and it's a great place to visit. Missed the fashion week in Paris? Fear not, the fashion week in Madrid is a big outlet for the fashion industry and for the nation's capital to show off its style. Basketball is a very popular sport in Spain, though soccer is without a doubt its most loved. In fact, it's hard to go anywhere in Spain without coming across something soccer related in one form or another. Historically speaking, soccer goes back over 100 years and it's had a long time to become part of Spanish culture. To date, Spain has not hosted a Women's World Cup, though it hosted the men's tournament back in 1982.

JORGE VILDA—A BRIEF COACHING PORTRAIT

Jorge Vilda was born in 1981 in Madrid, Spain. He has a massive task on his hands to navigate his team, a team with very little World Cup experience, into the elimination rounds. Doing that would be a great victory, to say the least. It should also go without saying that expectations on Spain's success are low. However, Vilda has a team under his guidance that was ranked number 12 in the world by FIFA prior to this tournament. So without a doubt, Vilda and Spain don't have the worst chance in the world to win the top honor in France, but it's highly doubtful.

KEY PLAYERS AND THEIR CHARACTERISTICS

Vicky Losado, Amanda Sampedro, and Jennifer Hermoso

Vicky Losado, born in 1991, is one of Spain's midfielders with experience playing in over 50 games with her national team. For Spain to find success, Losado should be active in the midfield, distributing the ball and finding a rhythm.

Amanda Sampedro is an attacking midfielder who's one of the higher scoring players with Spain. With over 40 appearances for her country, she's a player Spain is hoping will deliver as the tournament progresses.

Jennifer Hermoso is essentially regarded as a false 9 (which refers to a forward who tends to drop back into midfield a little or a lot, as opposed to a traditional number 9 forward who stays up top, in terms of positioning). During her time with the Spanish national team, she's tallied up a number of goals, and her scoring prowess will be needed in France for her team to have any realistic chance.

KEY PLAYER STATS

(Total career goals with their country)

	Games Played	Goals
Vicky Losado	54	13
Amanda Sampedro	42	11
Jennifer Hermoso	60	25

WHAT TO WATCH FOR ON TV—HOW MARTA, MORGAN, HEATH, AND OTHERS PLAY

Well, leading into World Cup 2019 Spain was ranked number 12 in the world by FIFA. It's a bit misleading, considering, and only considering, Spain's World Cup record to this point. Yet there's more. You can also take into account Spain's track record in European competitions and the Olympics, both of which are nonexistent. So one might ask: "Number 12 in the world? How far can that take you?" However, that's not to say that Spain does not have a talented team going into this tournament. In fact, who knows? Spain in 2019 could overcome all of its less-than-spectacular-past and really make something of this tournament. That is very possible. Though past success does have a lot to do with the present, at least according to some. To break through at the World Cup level is hard. Though if it's going to happen, if a team is going to have a breakout year in the World Cup, it has to happen at some time or another, and Spain is hoping that France 2019 will be its big year. Some of Spain's options include Marta

Corredera, Vicky Losado, Amanda Sampedro, Jennifer Hermoso, Silvia Meseguer, Alexia Putellas, Virginia Torrecilla, Patricia Guijarro, Andrea Pereira, Marta Torrejon, and Celia Jimenez Delgado.

Tactics and strategies: Can the Spanish women duplicate the tiki-taka style that the men's national team of Spain made so famous? That would be a difficult task for anyone, as the men's national team placed itself in rare air during what is called the "Golden Generation" in which Spain won the 2008 Euro, 2010 World Cup, and 2012 Euro in a row, with the tiki-taka style leading the way. (What is the tiki-taka style? Essentially, it is quick passing in short spaces between players in quick succession. This process repeats over and over again.) Critics like to jump in and point out that tiki-taka leads to nowhere. Proponents like to point out how it got Spain's men's national team three major championships in a row, a feat that no other European team has yet accomplished. As for the Spanish women duplicating tiki-taka and storming the castle of international women's soccer by first taking the 2019 World Cup: It might take some time to achieve the same results that the men did. However, for Spain's women's national team to have success in France 2019, it should indeed focus its attention on possession-oriented soccer, making this a high priority. Despite being ranked in a decent position by FIFA, Spain is definitely one of the underdogs in France.

Overall Team Ranking: 8.8
FIFA Ranking Going Into the World Cup: 12

SOUTH AFRICA

Twitter @Banyana_Banyana
World Cup titles: 0
Africa Women's Championships: 0

Known for:
A growing program
Desiree Ellis
Janine van Wyk

A BRIEF TEAM HISTORY

From 1991 to 2015, South Africa did not compete in a World Cup. This will be its very first one. Congratulations to South Africa! Making it this far is phenomenal, and it should be a great experience for South Africa to just be a part of the grand tournament, enjoy the process, and, not to mention, be a part of South African and World Cup history. Qualifying for France 2019 is definitely a big moment for women's soccer in South Africa. Historically, this should be looked at as a monumental first step in the right direction for women's soccer there, and a promise of future success for teams to come.

FACTS ABOUT THEIR COUNTRY

South Africa, which has a population of around 57 million people, operates with three capital cities: Pretoria (administrative/executive), Bloemfontein (judicial), and Cape Town (legislative). The women's soccer team has finished second place in the CAF Women's Championship (the Africa Women Cup of Nations) on five different occasions. The 2019 World Cup is the first World Cup appearance for the South African women's national team.

DESIREE ELLIS—A BRIEF COACHING PORTRAIT

Desiree Ellis was a midfielder and played a ton of games with Spurs Ladies of South Africa. She also played with the South African national team. Eventually, she transitioned to coaching South Africa beginning about 2016. Will South Africa win the 2019 World Cup? Slow down there, hoss. Talk about a challenge ahead for Ellis and company. In all likelihood, this tournament will serve as a learning experience for her team, and down the road South Africa may have better luck.

KEY PLAYERS AND THEIR CHARACTERISTICS

Janine van Wyk and Refiloe Jane

Janine van Wyk, born in 1987, has a ton of experience with South Africa as a midfielder, now pushing over 140 caps. She's a defender who's been playing with Houston Dash since 2017. She'll be a major asset for South Africa on defense, organizing and keeping scores against her team low, while distributing the ball and picking up possession for offensive success. As a leader on a team ranked number 48 in the world by FIFA prior to France 2019, it will be van Wyk's hope that her squad can keep to its game plan and push into the elimination rounds.

Refiloe Jane is a midfielder with South Africa looking to make big contributions in France 2019.

KEY PLAYER STATS
(Total career goals with their country)

	Games Played	Goals
Janine van Wyk	149	11
Refiloe Jane	62	5

WHAT TO WATCH FOR ON TV—HOW MARTA, MORGAN, HEATH, AND OTHERS PLAY

Janine van Wyk, Nothando Vilakazi, Refiloe Jane, Lebogang Ramalepe, Noko Matlou, Leandra Smeda, and Thembi Kgatlana are a few of South Africa's players who have gotten the team to this tournament in one way or another. As for making a splash in France 2019, that's another story.

Tactics and strategies: One strategy for the South Africans would be to hold on defensively for dear life and hope for ties. Another tactic might be to go all out and see what happens. As for formations, keeping it simple should be the best avenue for success, and a 4-4-2 would be the best bet for South Africa. Anything else could tamper with things—players might get confused, and games could get out of control. If anything, a 4-3-3 might be a better option as defensive pressure can be applied evenly throughout the field. But, it might be best after all for South Africa to go with a 4-4-2, and the comfort it offers with the two center mids working in tandem on defense. Expect to see a lot of counterattacking from South Africa. As a team ranked number 48 in the world, with all due respect, it's definitely not going to win this World Cup by out-possessing opponents with longwinded periods of possession for possession's sake. The counterattack will be key for success. But first it must keep a strong defense which will eventually intercept passes, attain loose balls, and kick-start the counter from there. Another focal point for South Africa will have to be in the set piece department. Hopefully, with counters working in its favor, South Africa can create chances around goal and possibly get a few free kicks here and there. Corner kicks will be another hopeful option for South Africa to capitalize on. But free kicks and corners are often lost causes, and a team needs many of them to occur throughout a game, pretty much on a regular basis, for the odds to work out. Basically, it's very hard to score on free kicks and corners, but it does happen from time to time, and South Africa will likely depend on these options for a foothold in games. It's a desperate measure, that's for sure, but it might just be the only advantage South Africa will have to stay in the tournament.

This is South Africa's first World Cup, so, given that it's an inexperienced team with no previous World Cup track record to build on, along with being a team that was ranked 48 in the world, some of the scores might get out of hand. But that's why the games are played, so they say.

Overall Team Ranking: 5.2
FIFA Ranking Going Into the World Cup: 48

AUSTRALIA

Twitter @TheMatildas
World Cup: 0
AFC Women's Asian Cup: 1

Known For
The nickname of the Matildas
A growing program
Alen Stajcic
Sam Kerr

A BRIEF TEAM HISTORY

Over time, Australia has been getting progressively better at the World Cup. In 1991, things didn't start out too great as Australia didn't qualify. During the World Cups of 1995, 1999, and 2003, Australia didn't get out of its group. Not great, but it's definitely better than not qualifying. In the World Cups of 2007, 2011, and 2015, Australia definitely improved from previous outings, but in each tournament, it was eliminated in the quarterfinals. Basically, it's been consistent improvement combined with consistent failure, an interesting place to be. Though, as history has shown, it has been an upward climb, one that has gotten closer to, rather than farther from, the semi-finals, which is a good thing.

As for the OFC Women's Nations Cup (the OFC Women's Championship), Australia has done rather well, winning it on three occasions while earning three second-place finishes as well. Australia has also won the AFC Women's Asian Cup in 2010. The Matildas have placed second in this tournament on three occasions.

FACTS ABOUT THEIR COUNTRY

Australia, a spectacular vacation destination, is known as the Land Down Under, a place where you can have a walkabout, see an Australian Rules Football game, or have a pint of Foster's all in one day. It has a population of around 25 million. Its capital city is Canberra, not Sydney (which is probably its most well-known city).

ALEN STAJCIC—A BRIEF COACHING PORTRAIT

Alen Stajcic, born in 1973, has been coaching the Australian women's side since 2014. Under his direction, Australia entered the 2019 World Cup ranked number 6 in the world. Not a bad place to be if you're the coach. Stajcic—a former midfielder with experience playing for Sutherland Sharks FC—has a strong challenge ahead in France. Should his side win the whole thing, Stajcic would be the first Australian coach to win a soccer World Cup.

KEY PLAYERS AND THEIR CHARACTERISTICS

Lisa De Vanna, Michelle Heyman, and Sam Kerr

Lisa De Vanna is a goal-scoring forward who has spread her talent around and played with numerous club teams ("numerous" would be putting it lightly). She's had stops with Orlando Pride, Washington Spirit, and Sydney FC, to name a few. With Australia, she's played in over 140 games with over 40 goals scored. If she remains uninjured, she should be a vital component to Australia's attack in France 2019.

Michelle Heyman has played forward with Australia since 2010. She's attained 20 goals, and she'll be looking for more in France 2019.

Sam Kerr, an attacking player to watch, has had stops recently with Chicago Red Stars and Sky Blue FC. Leading into the 2019 World Cup, FIFA listed Kerr as Australia's top player. As such, she'll be a key figure in Australia's game plan throughout the tournament.

KEY PLAYER STATS
(Total career goals with their country)

	Games Played	Goals
Lisa De Vanna	143	45
Michelle Heyman	61	20
Sam Kerr	72	27

WHAT TO WATCH FOR ON TV—HOW MARTA, MORGAN, HEATH, AND OTHERS PLAY

Lisa De Vanna, Michelle Heyman, Sam Kerr, Clare Polkinghorne, Laura Alleway, Elise Kellond-Knight, Alanna Kennedy, Chloe Logarzo, Emily van Egmond, Caitlin Foord, and Ellie Carpenter are a few of the players who will help Australia make a strong run in France 2019. Entering this tournament, FIFA ranked Australia at number 6 in the world, and, considering such a high ranking, the Matildas have every intention of lifting the trophy in the final game. This might be asking a lot. It is a program, mind you, that hasn't gotten to the semi-finals of a World Cup previous to this point. So taking a FIFA ranking of number 6 in the world and turning that into a magical World Cup championship in France might indeed be asking a lot. Though it's not out of the question.

Tactics and strategies: Perhaps utilizing a 4-3-3 or a 4-1-4-1, the Matildas can shake things up and pull off a few upsets for a history-making run this time around. Anything's possible. A few keys to success include free kicks, counterattacks, and strong defense. Australia will probably depend heavily on free kicks for many of its scoring opportunities. What this means is that it will first have to push the ball into enemy territory, somewhat forcefully, to gain ground, particularly around its opponent's goal, and look for fouls. Now, will Australia literally be looking for fouls, in other words, will diving become a factor? It's possible. But it's probably not the first thing Australian players will attempt. First, essentially what all this means is that Australia, a team with a lot of potential, one that is eager to reach the top, is a group that will likely push the tempo, which, in theory, should create fouls around the box (i.e., free kicks). Second, on top of that, Australia will certainly try to balance its attack with sound passing combinations in order to keep its opponent off the ball. The former can leave a team susceptible to counterattacks, which usually should be avoided. The latter is often a wise choice in the long run.

As Australia navigates though the tournament, it will be interesting to see how well it addresses some of these issues. France 2019 could be the big year for Australia, and the women from Down Under should definitely provide exciting games.

Overall Team Ranking: 9.4
FIFA Ranking Going Into the World Cup: 6

ITALY

Twitter @FIFAWWC*
World Cup titles: 0
European Championships: 0

Known for:
A program on the rise with high potential
Barbara Bonansea

A BRIEF TEAM HISTORY

Italy is a team working its way toward World Cup greatness. Though that may take a little time as it's a process. Things haven't exactly been spectacular so far, to say the least, but each new tournament offers a fresh start. In the 1991 World Cup, Italy made it to the quarterfinals where it was defeated 3-2 by Norway. Italy didn't qualify for World Cup 1995. At the 1999 World Cup, the Italians could not escape Group B, which included Brazil, Germany, and Mexico. From there things have gone downhill.

---

* A Twitter account for the women's national team of Italy could not be found. Instead, FIFA's Twitter account could possibly guide you to information about Italy's team.

For the 2003, 2007, 2011, and 2015 World Cups, Italy didn't get past the European qualifications. Now Italy's back, and World Cup 2019 is a great opportunity to change the past and really put a stamp on international soccer. It has a chance to get out to the races, take it to the other team, whoever that may be, make it worth playing for, and establish a piece of history for women's soccer in Italy. With a talented team led by its star player Barbara Bonansea, the sky is the limit, and France 2019 just might be the place where Italy surpasses its wildest expectations.

FACTS ABOUT THEIR COUNTRY

Italy—an amazingly complex historic place known for the Roman Empire, conquest, emperors, law, art, architecture, food, wine, engineering, fashion, beautiful cars, and so much more—is a unique Mediterranean nation with a population of approximately 60 million people. The nation's capital is Rome, where A.S. Roma Women plays its games. At the UEFA Women's Championship, the Italian women's soccer team has earned second place on two occasions.

MILENA BERTOLINI—A BRIEF COACHING PORTRAIT

Milena Bertolini, Italy's coach, may tinker with the formation. Italy has been seen using a 4-3-3 and 3-5-2, but perhaps something different altogether will be tossed into the mix. What's important is how the players play in the formation. Are they comfortable? Will the formation be a good avenue to team chemistry (i.e., will it assist with passing)? These are questions that Bertolini must address.

Another big question will be how to keep morale high, considering Italy's shaky past with the World Cup.

KEY PLAYERS AND THEIR CHARACTERISTICS

Barbara Bonansea, Elisa Bartoli, and Manuela Giugliano

Barbara Bonansea was listed by FIFA as the top Italian player prior to this World Cup. Bonansea is usually found out wide where she can wheel and deal. She's also known for putting balls in the back of the net. She's expected to do well for Italy this tournament, and, considering she was listed as Italy's top player, she has the added responsibility of putting Italy on the map, with a strong push into the elimination rounds.

Elisa Bartoli, born in 1991, is a defender who has experience with Roma, among other clubs. The 5'3" Bartoli should be found scurrying around the flanks, keeping things tidy on defense.

Manuela Giugliano, born in 1997, is a midfielder and has experience with A.C. Milan. Giugliano should be instrumental in organizing passing from midfield.

KEY PLAYER STATS
(Total career goals with their country)

	Games Played	Goals
Barbara Bonansea	37	14
Elisa Bartoli	35	1
Manuela Giugliano	48	21

WHAT TO WATCH FOR ON TV—HOW MARTA, MORGAN, HEATH, AND OTHERS PLAY

One way or another, Italy, who was ranked number 16 in the world leading into this World Cup, is going to try and upset a few teams while keeping its eyes on the grand prize: the World Cup final and championship trophy. This is a place the fabulous Italian women have never been; the men have won the World Cup four times, so it's fair to assume a title on the women's side would make Italians very pleased. En route to this goal, the Italian women might be seen using a 4-3-3 or a 3-5-2 or perhaps a variation. You never know!

Some of the players who helped guide Italy to the 2019 World Cup include Martina Rosucci, Daniela Sabatino, Daniela Stracchi, Melania Gabbiadini, Ilaria Mauro, Cristiana Girelli, Aurora Galli, Manuela Giugliano, Barbara Bonansea, Federica Di Criscio, Valentina Cernoia, Alia Guagni, Elena Linari, Sara Gama, Cecilia Salvai, and Elisa Bartoli.

Tactics and strategies: Patience. Does Italy have the skill and patience to use passing combinations to its advantage throughout the length of an entire game? Yes, possibly. First of all, yes it has the skill. Secondly, it might have the patience necessary to out-possess an opponent for an entire game. You have to remember that a soccer game goes by very quickly. They don't last very long. So to out-possess an opponent is a very important factor to success. The idea is: Don't let your opponent touch the ball, and you can get out of there with a win. Italy has the skill to do this. But it also requires a lot of patience to do such a thing, and, as is often the case, weaker teams at the World Cup level such as Italy—a program with a legacy of not doing super-great in previous World Cups—eventually lose the patience necessary to see a game through with confident possession-oriented soccer. If Italy can improve on this, good things should come its way.

Overall Team Ranking: 8.4
FIFA Ranking Going Into the World Cup: 16

BRAZIL

Twitter @FIFAWWC*
World Cup titles: 0
South American Championships: 7**

Known for:
Very passionate fans
Exciting games
Formiga
Marta

A BRIEF TEAM HISTORY

At World Cups, despite bringing an entertaining atmosphere to the game, Brazil has struggled a bit over the years. During the 1991 World Cup, Brazil couldn't get out of its group. Then at World Cup 1995, pretty much the same thing occurred when

---

* A Twitter account for the women's national team of Brazil could not be found. Instead, FIFA's Twitter account could possibly guide you to information about Brazil's team.

** Years ago this tournament was known as the South American Women's Football Championship, and now it's the Copa America Femenina.

Brazil still couldn't escape its group. Brazil did much better at the 1999 World Cup where it placed third overall. In 2003, Brazil lost out in the quarterfinals. World Cup 2007 represents Brazil's best so far; during that tournament, the team finished in second place. However, at the 2011 World Cup, Brazil lost again in the quarterfinals. And at the 2015 World Cup, things got worse for Brazil: It lost in the round of 16. Overall, not bad, but there's definitely room for improvement.

At the Olympics, Brazil has earned second place two times. In South America, Brazil has done very well. It has won Copa America Femenina (which was previously known as the South American Women's Football Championship) seven times. Brazil also has three championships from the Pan American Games.

FACTS ABOUT THEIR COUNTRY

Brazil has a population of around 210 million. Its capital is Brasilia, and its favorite sport, hands down, is soccer. The men's side, obviously, are world leaders, with five World Cup titles, along with numerous other accomplishments. The women's side has done very well in South America, and it has been making strides on the World Cup stage as well. Leading into the 2019 World Cup, Marta held the Brazilian women's record for goals scored with 110.

VADAO—A BRIEF COACHING PORTRAIT

Vadao, born in 1956 in Brazil, has coached over 25 teams; in some cases, he has coached a team more than once, but, nonetheless, Vadao has racked up an impressive coaching résumé, and he's likely not done. Currently, his task is to take Brazil to the final, win the World Cup, and add yet one more trophy to Brazil's overall winnings. He'll probably field the team in a 4-4-2, but don't be surprised to see another formation. With a talented group at his command, Vadao's Brazil should have some flair, mixed with sound structure on defense as the samba beat marches forward.

KEY PLAYERS AND THEIR CHARACTERISTICS

Marta Vieira da Silva, Thaisa de Moraes Rosa Moreno, Poliana Barbosa Medeiros, and Beatriz Zaneratto Joao

Always ready to dazzle you with nuanced South American skill, Marta is ready for yet another World Cup as she leads Brazil in France. She's considered by many to be the best female player of all time. For those who might disagree with such an assessment, they'd likely be quick to agree that she's in the upper echelon of greats alongside Mia Hamm, Michelle Akers, and Aly Wagner. As one of the superstars of women's soccer, she's still chasing that elusive World Cup title in France 2019.

Thaisa, a super-talented midfielder, has played with a number of clubs, including A.C. Milan Women. With Brazil, she's attained over 60 caps and is bringing this experience into France 2019 with the hope of leading Brazil to its first World Cup title.

Poliana Barbosa Medeiros is a defender who is taking a break from Orlando Pride to help Brazil lift the championship trophy at France 2019.

Beatriz Zaneratto Joao is an attacking player looking to make a big impression in France with goals and assists as Brazil finds its way through the tournament.

KEY PLAYER STATS
(Total career goals with their country)

	Games Played	Goals
Marta	133	110
Thaisa	64	4
Poliana Barbosa Medeiros	34	2
Beatriz Zaneratto Joao	49	13

WHAT TO WATCH FOR ON TV—HOW MARTA, MORGAN, HEATH, AND OTHERS PLAY

A few brilliant Brazilians that helped the team get to this point include Marta, Thaisa, Poliana Barbosa Medeiros, Beatriz Zaneratto Joao, Andressa Cavalari Machry, Camila, Monica, Tamires, Raquel Fernandes, and Debinha. Inspired by players like Formiga, Brazil is moving forward, hoping that this World Cup will be its first championship. On this quest, watch for a 4-4-2 formation (possibly a 4-3-3), as Brazil pulls out the tricks and surges ahead. The Brazilian team was ranked 10 in the world prior to France 2019. As such, it is among the top teams with a little room for improvement. It's assumed Brazil will get past its group. However, in the elimination rounds, will Brazil be good enough to get past the quarterfinals? Considering Marta might not be as quick as she once was, this might be a challenge.

Tactics and strategies: Brazil must have other players rise to the level of Marta, create a pulse in midfield, and implement defenders into the attack. Marta, though, will still be affective. As the central focus of the attack in past years, Marta has carried the team, but she can't do it forever. Brazil will need auxiliary players to step up and take responsibility for the team and to surge forward so that everything is not riding on whether or not Marta can deliver solo brilliance. In doing so, team chemistry should begin to click on all cylinders, and Brazil will be in a great position to succeed. Almost certainly, Brazil should get out of its group. However, after that, in the elimination rounds, things will get tricky.

If Brazil can create some magic in midfield from the beginning of the tournament, then it can build on momentum by the round of 16, at which point, watch out. If Brazil has everything flowing in a creative direction, the tournament could get very interesting very fast. But, initially, the Brazilians need to find the samba beat with solid midfield play, and the best way to achieve this is to implement the two-man game. This is essentially a very simple connection between two players passing the ball. In essence, it's passing the ball right back to the teammate that just passed to you. So if Marta receives a pass from Beatriz and passes it right back to Beatriz, then the two-man game has been established. The more this is repeated throughout the field, the better it is for team chemistry. Should Brazil's midfielders get passing connections like this going early in the tournament, then confidence will build, and magical play will likely occur.

Brazil must implement its defenders into the attack. When Brazil does this, the whole attack begins to operate on a higher level. So it is crucial for Brazilian defenders to join the attack as often as possible to create different scoring chances from the point of view of the opposing team. Throwing defenders forward, particularly outside defenders, always throws off the other team. If Brazil can use its outside defenders in the attack, and even toss in a central defender from time to time, it will have very good results.

Overall Team Ranking: 9.1
FIFA Ranking Going Into the World Cup: 10

JAMAICA

Twitter @jff_football
World Cup titles: 0
North American Championships: 0

Known for:
Nickname: Reggae Girlz
Being the first Caribbean team to play in a Women's World Cup
Chinyelu Asher
Lauren Silver

A BRIEF TEAM HISTORY

Jamaica is a growing program, one with potential. It's a program on the move. After all, this is the first World Cup the Jamaica women—known as the Reggae Girlz—have entered. For women's soccer in Jamaica, and that of the greater Caribbean region, this is a huge, historic moment. Outside of qualifying for France 2019, the biggest achievement from the Reggae Girlz would be getting third place at the 2018 CONCACAF Women's Championship, which was held in the United States.

FACTS ABOUT THEIR COUNTRY

Jamaica is a beautiful vacation destination island in the Caribbean (just south of Cuba) with a population of approximately 2.8 million people. Jamaicans love their soccer along with track and field (particularly the sprinting events). France 2019 is the first World Cup the Jamaican women have qualified for. Fans watching the games on TV from Jamaica will likely have Red Stripe beer to celebrate with.

HUE MENZIES—A BRIEF COACHING POR-TRAIT

As FIFA's website pointed out prior to France 2019, Hue Menzies led this team to become the first Caribbean side to qualify for a Women's World Cup. Though, his team's challenge is far from over. Menzies has a huge task on his hands. How can he take Jamaica, an underdog team of epic proportions, and somehow win the World Cup in France? The better question might be one of a simpler nature, and that would be: How can he take Jamaica, an underdog team of epic proportions, and somehow get out of the group stage? The latter, to say the least, would be a huge achievement for the Reggae Girlz. The former would be a groundbreaking miracle. After all, going into France 2019, FIFA had Jamaica ranked number 53 in the world.

KEY PLAYERS AND THEIR CHARACTERISTICS

Chinyelu Asher and Lauren Silver

Chinyelu Asher was born in 1993 in the United States; her dad is Jamaican and was a soccer player at Howard University in Washington D.C., which would be Chinyelu's connection with Jamaica. She's a midfielder expected to help the Reggae Girlz make a splash in France 2019.

Lauren Silver, born in 1993, is a midfielder with experience from the University of Florida's soccer team and recently from Glasgow City in Scotland. She's looking to have a good tournament in France 2019 and hopefully push Jamaica into the elimination rounds.

KEY PLAYER STATS

(Total career goals with their country)

	Games Played	Goals
Chinyelu Asher	20	3
Lauren Silver	18	0

WHAT TO WATCH FOR ON TV—HOW MARTA, MORGAN, HEATH, AND OTHERS PLAY

Chinyelu Asher, Lauren Silver, Konya Plummer, Dominique Bond-Flasza, Allyson Swaby, Toriana Patterson, Marlo Sweatman, and Khadija Shaw are a few of the players who helped get Jamaica to this point.

Prior to this World Cup, FIFA had ranked Jamaica number 53 in the world. Keep an eye out for a team with nothing to lose. Just getting to France 2019 was a victory, plain and simple. Though, it would seem likely that Jamaica will go all out in the group stage, hoping for a small miracle to advance into the elimination rounds. Though, it would be very difficult for such a thing to happen, and to do so would require a lot of good fortune. Jamaica, Chile, and South Africa are in a similar situation. Each team is playing for pride, experience, and an opportunity to get noticed by club teams looking to sign a few new players.

Tactics and strategies: Since Jamaica is a very new team to the World Cup experience, it should play to win and see what happens. Throw the kitchen sink at opponents in the group stage and maybe something crazy will happen, like somehow advancing to the round of 16. Jamaica might as well go full-on offense and never look back. Or, the Jamaican women could play in a defensive shell, be very tentative, and hope for the best. But what would be the point? Being as low ranked as Jamaica is, no matter what it does, a few things are bound to happen. Jamaica will probably get outplayed, and the score could get out of hand. So, in essence, let loose and go for it. (With that said, a strong defense is still necessary, and the Jamaican players should remember this at all times.)

Furthermore, with every opportunity there is, an attempt at counterattacking down the wings should be made, *while also utilizing the center of the field with strategic passing.* Too many underdog teams get caught up with "exploiting the wings" for some kind of "advantage." Usually that's a bunch of nonsense, and it merely isolates players out in the middle of nowhere, with nowhere to go on top of that. You see, the wings might be open for brief periods of time, but there's a simple drawback to always getting players out wide: The line is out of bounds, and experienced defenders take advantage of this; in essence, the line turns into another defender. Utilize the middle as often as possible, even in counterattacks; this can't be stressed enough.

However Jamaica's World Cup tour ends up, one thing is definitely going to be left behind and that will be the groundwork laid down for future Jamaican teams to follow. It has to be remembered that when a team qualifies for a World Cup for the first time, that carries with it an underlying feeling that it's *also* a team that might not be back for a while. Maybe this will be the case, maybe it won't. Jamaica might, in fact, turn around and qualify for the next three World Cups in a row. You never know. Usually, with a small country like Jamaica, it depends on a particular generation of players at a particular time. Once an older generation begins to retire, then it's the responsibility of a new generation of players to pick up where things left off, and this is hit or miss. Some generations are simply better than others. In this regard, often times, small countries like Jamaica have to hope for the best. Fans of Jamaican soccer certainly hope this generation of players will have a great showing in France and have continued success for the next 10 years, at least.

Overall Team Ranking: 5 leaning on 4.7
FIFA Ranking Going Into the World Cup: 53

ENGLAND

Twitter @Lionesses
World Cup titles: 0
European Championships: 0

Known for:
Nickname: Three Lionesses
Phil Neville
Hope Powell
Karen Walker
Kelly Smith
Casey Stoney
Rachel Yankey
Fara Williams
Eniola Aluko
Alex Scott
Karen Carney
Steph Houghton

A BRIEF TEAM HISTORY

The Women's World Cup for England has been a rocky road, to say the least. In 1991, England didn't compete. In 1995, England qualified but lost in the quarterfinals. For the World Cups of 1999 and 2003, qualification was again not in the cards for England. Things got better at World Cups 2007 and 2011, as England qualified and made it to the quarterfinals in both tournaments. The best year for the Three Lionesses came in 2015, at the World Cup in Canada. England finished third place overall, and it's now looking to build on that momentum going into France 2019.

The best results for England in European competition have come in the form of two second-place finishes, including the 1984 European Competition for Women's Football and the UEFA Women's Euro in 2009.

FACTS ABOUT THEIR COUNTRY

England, the cradle of soccer, has a population of around 55 million people. England's women's national soccer team has not won a World Cup yet. The men's national soccer team of England won one World Cup title in 1966. England has not yet hosted a Women's World Cup. As of 2019, Fara Williams* leads the England national team with caps, with 168. In second place is Alex Scott, with 140. As of January 2019, Karen Carney** is in third place, closing in on Alex Scott.

---

* She is still playing.
** She is still playing.

PHIL NEVILLE—A BRIEF COACHING PORTRAIT

Phil Neville, a longtime member of Manchester United and Everton, who also played many years with England, has taken the responsibility of leading England's Three Lionesses to World Cup glory. Can he do it? Can he claim the first Women's World Cup title for England? He's gotten the team off to a good start. In fact, just prior to France 2019, FIFA had England ranked at number 4 worldwide.

KEY PLAYERS AND THEIR CHARACTERISTICS

Steph Houghton, Ellen White, and Toni Duggan

Steph Houghton, born in 1988, is a central defender who currently plays club ball with Manchester City. As captain of England, she's going to be critical in organizing the defense, distributing the ball from the back, and keeping morale high.

Ellen White, born in 1989, is a forward who has played with England since 2010. She has over 70 caps, with a scoring touch to boot, and her expertise should be vital for England's success in France 2019.

Toni Duggan, born in Liverpool, England, is a goal-scoring threat England will be counting on for putting balls into the back of the net.

KEY PLAYER STATS

(Total career goals with their country)

	Games Played	Goals
Steph Houghton	100	11
Ellen White	75	26
Toni Duggan	66	22

WHAT TO WATCH FOR ON TV—HOW MARTA, MORGAN, HEATH, AND OTHERS PLAY

A few of the brilliant players who have helped get England to this point include Steph Houghton, Ellen White, Toni Duggan, Fran Kirby, Nikita Parris, Melissa Lawley, Jodie Taylor, Keira Walsh, Georgia Stanway, Lucy Staniforth, the highly capped Jill Scott, Jade Moore, Izzy Christiansen, Karen Carney, Leah Williamson, Demi Stokes, Abbie McManus, Alex Greenwood, Gabrielle George, Rachel Daly, Lucy Bronze, Millie Bright, Hannah Blundell, Carly Telford, Ellie Roebuck, Mary Earps, and Karen Bardsley. This could be England's year; it just might be on the road to victory. Possibly going with a 4-3-3 or perhaps a 4-1-4-1, the team is strong and ready for all challenges ahead. Confidence is high as England was ranked number 4 in the world by FIFA prior to the tournament.

Tactics and strategies: England can't rush things and mustn't worry about scoring goals, and the midfielders must involve everyone. What could hold England back? For starters, rushing things will not be a friend of the Three Lionesses. Composure in the back, coupled with solid distribution to the flanks and throughout the midfield should be a task England keeps its eye on. Sometimes it's easy to rush. This is especially true for a team like England, one that takes itself seriously. When a team thinks highly of itself, it becomes easy to get agitated against less talented competition. The superior team starts thinking negative thoughts: *We need to score. Why haven't we scored? We should've scored by now. Are we going to score? How much time is left?* When this starts happening, it's a potential recipe for disaster. At this point, the superior team begins rushing play in an all-out attempt to score. What needs to happen is almost the complete opposite. If the superior players are not scoring, there shouldn't be a feeling of anxiety. Rather, they should feel relaxed. Obviously, a little urgency is good. But if a team can remain relaxed and concentrated on fundamentals, then better things should arrive in the scoring department. Fundamentals are twofold. Defensively, the players must be thinking about anticipating tackles and getting loose balls. Offensively, the players must be thinking about finding opportunities to dribble, passing combinations, and by keeping the thoughts simple, scoring chances will gradually become more abundant.

When England plays a team of equal talent, the same approach should apply. However, it should be said, and this is an interesting phenomenon in sports, in games with an equally talented participant, it's often easy to forget to be anxious. Players get wrapped up in the moment, and the game simply flows. Why is this? Against a good opponent, one that is equally talented or even a little better, players realize that scoring opportunities are hard to come by; this causes players to be "in the game" or "in the zone," and not constantly worrying about scoring. Instead, the players begin thinking about moment-to-moment plays in the game. (This is good; psychologically, this is where a team needs to be.) Against a weaker, less talented opponent, players get that agitated feeling when goals aren't piling up. (This is not good; psychologically, this is a bad place to be.)

Somehow, England must be satisfied with just playing the game well, and goals will come from there. England might get rattled if goals aren't happening, but the best course of action will be to stay composed and relaxed, and goals will arrive more frequently with this approach.

The midfielders must involve everyone. If the midfielders can successfully distribute the ball and get everyone involved, then good things should show up on the scoreboard. However, this is easier said than done. What exactly does getting everyone involved mean? In England's case, it means having the center midfielders push the ball from wing to wing with the intent of getting it right back. Being a "one-pass wonder" will not do England any good this tournament. A pass needs to be made by a center mid to an outside mid, and immediately that center mid who just passed the ball needs to follow the pass and become available for a return pass. Now, it goes without saying, that a return pass might not be the best option every time. (And that's fine.) Though, it needs to be an option, nonetheless. From there, hopefully, the outside mid can pass the ball right back to the center mid, which creates chemistry and passing combinations; hence, England's offensive game at large will flow much better from that passing connection.

The center mid getting a return pass from an outside mid is just one example. The center mids need to be doing this with as many teammates as possible, defenders and, obviously, forwards included. It's a lot to ask of center mids, but, then again, this is part of the responsibility of the position. An important part of

England's overall offensive approach is to get the center mids active in distributing the ball this way. It opens up passing lanes throughout the duration of a game. England has not succeeded efficiently in this department in the past; otherwise it would have had a World Cup title by now. It's a program with high quality, and tons of promise—and it needs to deliver. And quite frankly, it can deliver. The only thing holding England back is England.

In the end, England's success depends on players not rushing things, not worrying about scoring, and actively distributing the ball from midfield.

Overall Team Ranking: 9.6
FIFA Ranking Going Into the World Cup: 4

SCOTLAND

Twitter @ScotWFootball
World Cup titles: 0
European Championships: 0

Known for:
Shelley Kerr
Rachel Corsie
Jane Ross

A BRIEF TEAM HISTORY

Scotland has a women's national team that is on the move, improving all the time. Things didn't get off to a great start for the women of Scotland, though. "Scotland's first official match, a 3-2 defeat to England, took place in November 1972."[9] Frankly, since then, things haven't gotten much better. In fact, World Cup 2019 in France is the first for Scotland's women. Without a doubt, looking at Scotland's overall record, qualifying for France would have to be its biggest accomplishment; this would be the improvement from previous years, and, for the sake of Scotland's soccer program, this could be the start of something great. But let's not get too excited and expect Scotland to win a World Cup in the next 20 years. Give it some time. By time, possibly give it 36, 54, or 72 years…

FACTS ABOUT THEIR COUNTRY

The Scots reside in a geographic region just north of England. Scotland's capital city is Edinburgh, and the country's population is around 5.4 million.

SHELLEY KERR—A BRIEF COACHING PORTRAIT

Shelley Kerr, born in 1969, is a former defender with experience playing with Scotland's national team. Now she has the unenviable task of leading Scotland to a World Cup championship. Scotland has used a 4-2-3-1 in the past. Whether this remains the case is yet to be seen. Overall, regardless what formation Kerr places on the field, it's going to be an uphill battle for Scotland throughout the whole tournament—should it get out of the group stage, that is. Without a doubt, for a program that's never been to the World Cup, it would be an absolute victory to escape into the elimination rounds.

KEY PLAYERS AND THEIR CHARACTERISTICS

Rachel Corsie, Joanne Love, and Jane Ross

Rachel Corsie, born in 1989, is the captain and defender of Scotland assigned with the task of leading this team into foreign territory: a World Cup. That's right. As the first World Cup for the Scottish women's national team, Corsie and company have an enormous challenge on their hands, and the competition will be fierce.

Joanne Love has participated in over 180 games for Scotland, and she's bound to reach 200. Watch for her in the midfield as she provides balance and guidance for the Scots.

Jane Ross is a prolific goal-scorer and one to watch as Scotland challenges for a World Cup title.

KEY PLAYER STATS
(Total career goals with their country)

	Games Played	Goals
Rachel Corsie	101	16
Joanne Love	187	13
Jane Ross	122	57

WHAT TO WATCH FOR ON TV—HOW MARTA, MORGAN, HEATH, AND OTHERS PLAY

Rachel Corsie, Joanne Love, Jane Ross, Claire Emslie, Erin Cuthbert, Lana Clelland, Fiona Brown, Caroline Weir, Christie Murray, Hayley Lauder, Leanne Crichton, Lizzie Arnot, Kirsty Smith, Joelle Murray, Nicola Docherty, Frankie Brown, Jennifer Beattie, and Chloe Arthur are a few field players who got Scotland to this point. It's a team that will be making its debut for Scotland in the World Cup, and not much is expected to happen in terms of making a big run in the tournament. Fans and critics alike would most likely agree that in order for Scotland to win the World Cup outright, it will take something of a small miracle. With that said, an underdog team like Scotland is usually fun to watch; the pressure is off, and a team of this sort can really give it a go and have a run at opposing teams, making for very interesting soccer.

Tactics and strategies: Scotland should embrace the underdog role, limit long-ball soccer, and try to establish dominance in the middle of the field. Scotland should most definitely embrace being an underdog and let loose, have a run at opponents, and really just play the game. If Scotland, instead, begins worrying about results, then it will likely depart France 2019 very early. The Scots should definitely not rely on long-ball tactics. This is old-school soccer from the dark ages of the 1980s and before. At times if a team finds itself down a goal or two it will instinctively resort to long-ball soccer. Players will start chipping the ball down field, and they'll quickly begin launching chaotic crosses into the box with a hope and a prayer. These are signs of desperation.

Scotland will find success by using the center of the field with strategic passing. The mindset of most teams from the British Isles is to get the ball out wide. Well, if this is a tactic to be used, it should be understood that the best way to achieve dominance out wide is to actively involve players in the middle of the field because these are often the players that provide distribution out wide in the first place. Should Scotland find a balance in these areas, good things might eventually come its way this tournament.

Overall Team Ranking: 8
FIFA Ranking Going Into the World Cup: 20

ARGENTINA

Twitter @FIFAWWC*
World Cup titles: 0
South American Championships: 1

Known for:
A program on the rise
Carlos Borrello
Estefania Banini

A BRIEF TEAM HISTORY

Argentina is known for a big 11-0 loss it took from Germany in 2007. Not a good game for Argentina. On the flip side, Argentina's biggest victory would be that of 12-0 after dishing it out to Bolivia back in 1995.

As for World Cups, Argentina has been finding its way. Argentina did not compete in the 1991, 1995, or 1999 World Cups. In World

---

* A Twitter account for the women's national team of Argentina could not be found. Instead, FIFA's Twitter account could possibly guide you to information about Argentina's team.

Cup 2003, Argentina finally qualified. However, in Group C (which also included Germany, Canada, and Japan), it finished dead last. Then came the 2007 World Cup. Argentina was in Group A (alongside Germany, England, and Japan), whereby, yet again, it finished dead last. Coincidentally, this was the time Argentina lost to Germany by the score of 11-0. In the 2011 and 2015 World Cups, Argentina was nowhere to be found. The 2019 FIFA Women's World Cup offers Argentina a whole new lease on life in international competition. Perhaps, just maybe, Argentina can find a little redemption.

Argentina won the South American Women's Football Championship in 2006.

FACTS ABOUT THEIR COUNTRY

Argentina—a beautiful country in South America—has a population of around 43 million people. Its capital city is Buenos Aires, and the county's most popular sport, by far, is soccer. The men's national team of Argentina has two World Cup titles, while the women's team is working its way toward greatness. As fans cheer on the women's team in France 2019, a few beers that might be tossed around include Quilmes and Antares Kolsch.

CARLOS BORRELLO—A BRIEF COACHING PORTRAIT

Carlos Borrello is a coach who might have the toughest task at hand in the whole tournament this year. After all, he's leading a women's team that, like it or not, has to live up to the Argentinian men's record (which is world class). And so far, the Argentinian women's team hasn't done very well, especially in World Cups. Borrello has been with the women's team during the good times and the bad; he's been there and is looking to turn things around with this opportunity in France.

KEY PLAYERS AND THEIR CHARACTERISTICS

Maria Belen Potassa, Estefania Banini, and Yamila Rodriguez

Maria Belen Potassa, born in 1988, is representing a team that is looking to get Argentina on the map at the World Cup level. As a forward, she'll be seeking opportunities to dribble around the box and create scoring chances. She can't do it alone. As a group, Argentina needs to put her in the best positions for success.

Estefania Banini, born in 1990, has experience playing in the US with Washington Spirit. Going into France 2019, FIFA named her the top player of Argentina. She'll be pivotal in Argentina's attack, creating play with the dribble, looking for telling passes, and pushing toward goal, hoping to put a few in the back of the net.

Yamila Rodriguez is a young, up-and-coming forward to keep an eye on.

KEY PLAYER STATS

(Total career goals with their country)

	Games Played	Goals
Maria Belen Potassa	13	5
Estefania Banini	6	6
Yamila Rodriguez	4	0

WHAT TO WATCH FOR ON TV—HOW MARTA, MORGAN, HEATH, AND OTHERS PLAY

A few Argentinian players who have helped get the team to this point include Florencia Bonsegundo, Estefania Banini, Maria Belen Potassa, Yamila Rodriguez, Amancay Urbani, Vanesa Santana, Mariana Larroquette, Virginia Gomez, Mariana Gaitan, Mariela Coronel, Micaela Cabrera, and Agustina Barroso.

Tactics and strategies: Argentina will need to use defensive shape and counterattacks. Will Argentina be able to hold off the avalanche of offensive power from its opposition? Will Argentina have another 11-0 defeat like the one it suffered against Germany in the 2007 World Cup? This 2019 World Cup is a big test for the Argentinians. This is, quite simply, an opportunity to rewrite its women's soccer history with a fantastic performance in France. This will start with Argentina focusing all its efforts on organization in its defensive backline. Argentina must keep good defensive shape, and, on top of that, it must be mindful of one-on-one battles. If Argentina can stay focused and win individual defensive battles, then good things might come its way. First, and this is important to reiterate, Argentina must have good defensive shape, and if this is accomplished then one-on-one individual battles will come out in its favor more often than not.

Argentina needs to focus on counterattacks for any hope of moving forward throughout this tournament. Good counterattacking starts with good defending. So, therefore, if Argentina keeps good defensive shape, then plenty of counterattacking opportunities should theoretically open up. It's a balance that Argentina must find for any kind of success in France.

In Argentina, in many cases, soccer is bigger than life itself. While the men's team is expected to win each and every World Cup, the women's side is allowed room to breathe, and, the general consensus is "hopefully they can get out of their group." The women's team from Argentina is part of a program that is gaining a foothold in international soccer. To put it politely, Argentina is a team that is up against it. With its past World Cup record, Argentina is a good team for other teams to have in their group, an easy win so to speak. But, under coach Borrello, and the ups and downs he's had with the team over the years, Argentina is looking to usher in a new era for the women of South America.

Overall Team Ranking: 6.4
FIFA Ranking Going Into the World Cup: 36

JAPAN

Twitter @FIFAWWC*
World Cup titles: 1
AFC Women's Asian Cup: 2**

Known for:
A World Cup championship
A strong program
Technically sound players
Exciting games
Homare Sawa
Aya Miyama

A BRIEF TEAM HISTORY

When it comes to the World Cup, Japan has done well very recently. In the beginning there were challenges, and things weren't going so well, but over time things came around.

---

*   A Twitter account for the women's national team of Japan could not be found. Instead, FIFA's Twitter account could possibly guide you to information about Japan's team.

** Outside of the AFC Women's Asian Cup, Japan has won other Asian competitions. See "A Brief Team History" for more.

At the first World Cup in 1991, Japan didn't make it out of its group. At the 1995 World Cup, Japan improved and made it to the quarterfinals. Then, for the next three World Cups (1999, 2003, and 2007), Japan didn't get out of its group.

By the time of the 2011 World Cup, things were drastically different; the Cup was held in Germany, and this was the year Japan would make its move. Led by the illustrious Homare Sawa, Japan started out in Group B with England, Mexico, and New Zealand. With two wins and a loss (the loss delivered by England), Japan eventually placed second behind England. During the quarterfinals, Japan defeated the talented Germans 1-0. Next up, Japan took down Sweden in the semi-finals, 3-1. At that moment, Japan had arrived. During the final—held in Frankfurt, Germany—Japan defeated the United States in a penalty-kick shootout for the title.

Japan wasn't done. The Japanese had another brilliant showing at the 2015 World Cup, held in Canada. Initially, in Group C, Japan had a relatively easy draw against Cameroon, Switzerland, and Ecuador. It won each game by a one-goal margin and won the group. In the round of 16, Japan started out with a 2-1 victory over the Netherlands. During the quarterfinals, Japan faced a tough challenge against Australia, but in the end, left the field with a 1-0 win. Japan kept its one-goal margin going against England in the semi-finals with a 2-1 win. And so it was: two final appearances in a row. Japan had reached the championship game yet again, and, low and behold, the United States was waiting for a rematch after 2011. This time around, Japan wasn't so lucky. The United States went into lift-off mode and won the game—and its third World Cup title—5-2. Japan earned second place and began looking ahead to France 2019.

Japan won the AFC Women's Asian Cup in 2014 and 2018. Japan has also won first place at the Asian Games in 2010 and 2018. In addition, Japan won the EAFF Women's Football Championship in 2008 and 2010 and earned second place at the 2012 Olympics.

FACTS ABOUT THEIR COUNTRY

Japan, a beautiful island nation in the Pacific, has a population of around 126 million people. Its capital is Tokyo, which is known as one of the cleanest big cities in the world. The most caps for the women's national team of Japan goes to Homare Sawa, with 205. Who has the most goals for the women's team of Japan? You guessed it, the one and only, Homare Sawa; she holds the record with 83.

ASAKO TAKAKURA-TAKEMOTO—A BRIEF COACHING PORTRAIT

Asako Takakura-Takemoto, born in 1968, was a midfielder with the Japanese women's team, and now she leads from the sideline. Japan is heading into France 2019 with an ultra-talented group, not to mention with the experience of two finals appearances in World Cups 2011 and 2015. There's a lot of momentum to build on there, and Asako Takakura-Takemoto is in a great position to deliver Japan another World Cup title.

KEY PLAYERS AND THEIR CHARACTERISTICS

Yui Hasegawa, Saori Ariyoshi, Yuika Sugasawa, and Mana Iwabuchi

Yui Hasegawa, born in 1997, is a young midfielder whose career is going to be worth watching. She has plenty of experience with Nippon TV Beleza and will be looking to utilize her playing and passing skills in France 2019.

Saori Ariyoshi is an experienced defender looking to hold the fort for Japan on its quest to another World Cup title. As a member of the 2015 World Cup All-Star Team, she's not a big goal-scorer with Japan but adds depth in the back, which helps set the rest of the team in motion.

Yuika Sugasawa, born in 1990, is a talented forward with experience from the 2015 World Cup. She has over 15 goals for Japan and is a player to watch.

Mana Iwabuchi was listed by FIFA as Japan's top player going into France 2019. She has past World Cup experience along with a wealth of knowledge she's acquired from the women's club teams of INAC Kobe Leonessa, Bayern Munich, TSG 1899 Hoffenheim, and Nippon TV Beleza. She's a player with skill and other teams should be weary of her presence around the box where she and her teammates will work with combination passing and tenacity to create good scoring chances. As a result, Iwabuchi should likely be a key figure for Japan throughout the tournament.

KEY PLAYER STATS

(Total career goals with their country)

	Games Played	Goals
Yui Hasegawa	30	4
Saori Ariyoshi	63	1
Yuika Sugasawa	60	17
Mana Iwabuchi	61	20

WHAT TO WATCH FOR ON TV—HOW MARTA, MORGAN, HEATH, AND OTHERS PLAY

A few players who have helped Japan to this point include Yui Hasegawa, Saori Ariyoshi, Yuika Sugasawa, Mana Iwabuchi, the experienced Aya Sameshima, Moeno Sakaguchi, Shiori Miyake, Risa Shimizu, Nana Ichise, Mizuho Sakaguchi, Rumi Utsugi, Emi Nakajima, Hina Sugita, Narumi Miura, Fuka Nagano, Hinata Miyazawa, Kumi Yokoyama, Yuka Momiki, Mina Tanaka, and Saki Kumagai (the captain). Should Japan reach the final game, it would be for the third time in a row. With Japan's technical approach, sound passing, organized defense, and solid organization, it wouldn't be out of the question to see Japan holding the championship trophy yet again. On its quest to regaining the world title, don't be surprised to see a 4-4-1-1 (which essentially is a 4-4-2) or a 4-4-2.

Tactics and strategies: Japan must dominate the midfield, and it must have its forwards actively involved in possession. Japan has reached a level of success recently by using skill, technique, and overall organization to its advantage. The latter would be referring to both the offensive and defensive sides of the ball. The way Japan has achieved harmony is with intelligent midfield play.

During this tournament, Japan must stay consistent and do what it does best. If, and only if, everything can flow through its midfield, then Japan could theoretically find offensive balance throughout the 2019 World Cup. This requires its midfielders to be active by way of looking for passing combinations all over the field. Here's the tricky part: The midfielders can't do it alone. There has to be a conscious effort by everyone involved to get the ball to the feet of the midfielders as often as possible and with a good rhythm. The rhythm has to be artistically correct so the midfielders can turn with the ball comfortably. (Just passing the ball to midfielders frequently is not enough; the rhythm of a pass, not to mention the touch of a pass, is often more important than anything else; if a pass is slightly too hard, or played at the last second, then it might create more problems for the midfielder than anything else.) So it's imperative that Japan's defenders are in sync with one another. They can achieve this by establishing a confident possession game. Once this is achieved, then intelligent passes, with good rhythm and touch, can be played successfully to the midfielders. At this point, Japan will be close to "all parts working together in harmony."

In order for Japan's midfielders to be in offensive harmony with the defenders, the forwards have to play a crucial role in making appropriate supporting runs to establish passing connections. Once the forwards establish good checking runs, then passing lanes should open. This requires the forwards to play with their backs to the goal. It requires focus, patience, and simple passes. If the forwards can combine dribbling prowess here and there, it would be very beneficial for the overall success of the offense.

There's a certain skill in finding a balance between knowing when to pass and when to dribble. But, if done correctly, a balance is achieved, and the offense can flow much more productively as a result. This all starts with a lot of movement from the forwards by supporting the mids and defenders during bouts of possession.

Japan is one of the top teams in the world, and it will play exciting, high-quality games.

Overall Team Ranking: 9.4
FIFA Ranking Going Into the World Cup: 8

CANADA

Twitter @CanadaSoccerEN
World Cup titles: 0
North American Championships: 2

Known for:
Christine Sinclair
Charmaine Hooper
Silvana Burtini
Diana Matheson
Rhian Wilkinson
Sophie Schmidt
Desiree Scott

A BRIEF TEAM HISTORY

Canada's relationship with the World Cup has been hit or miss, with emphasis on the latter. Canada didn't compete in the 1991 World Cup. In 1995 and 1999, Canada qualified for the World Cup but was eliminated in its group. World Cup 2003 was Canada's best as it placed fourth overall. Then, for the World Cups of 2007 and 2011, Canada couldn't get out of its group. As for the 2015 World Cup, which Canada hosted, it progressed to the quarterfinals where it lost to England.

Outside of the World Cup, the large country up north has had better luck. To its credit, Canada won the 1998 CONCACAF Women's Championship. It also won the 2010 CONCACAF Women's World Cup Qualifying tournament. In addition, Canada won the 2011 Pan American Games, along with three championships from the Cyprus Women's Cup (2008, 2010, and 2011), one championship from the 2016 Algarve Cup, and one championship from the 2015 Four Nations Tournament.

Not bad for a program still trying to get into the top three of a World Cup.

FACTS ABOUT THEIR COUNTRY

Canada's capital city is not Montreal, Toronto, or Vancouver. It's Ottawa, and the nation's population is approximately 37 million. Some Canadian beers that fans might enjoy while watching the 2019 World Cup on TV include Molson Canadian, Moosehead Lager, and Labatt Blue.

If you think Canada's big 12-0 win over Cuba in October 2018 was something, check this: Canada defeated Puerto Rico 21-0 back in 1998. Now that's a victory. As of January 23, 2019, Christine Sinclair had the most caps for Canada, with 275, and the most goals, with 178.

KENNETH HEINER-MOLLER—A BRIEF COACHING PORTRAIT

As Canada's coach, Kenneth Heiner-Moller, who was born in 1971, might deliver a 4-2-3-1 or possibly a 4-3-3. He's guiding a team that's done very well recently, having received second place in the 2018 CONCACAF Women's Championship. In fact, Heiner-Moller is sitting in a pretty good position as FIFA had ranked Canada at number 5 in the world prior to this World Cup. Under Heiner-Moller, this might be the year Canada brings home the big prize.

KEY PLAYERS AND THEIR CHARACTERISTICS

Christine Sinclair, Desiree Scott, and Ashley Lawrence

Christine Sinclair, the one and only, leads all Canadian teammates in caps and goals. The goal-scoring phenom has been with the Canadian national team since 2000 and is still going strong. Her team in France 2019 was ranked number 5 in the world by FIFA prior to the tournament, which is a good place to be. With this momentum, Canada is looking to make a big move this tournament with Sinclair at the forefront.

Desiree Scott is a midfielder who won't be accused of being a goal-scoring diva. In fact, since 2010, she's played in over 135 games for Canada without scoring a goal. However, she's a midfielder who keeps things in order and leaves the scoring for others. She recently joined Utah Royals FC. With her club and national team experience, Scott is looking to guide Canada in a positive direction in France 2019.

Ashley Lawrence, born in 1995, has gained experience recently with Paris Saint-Germain Feminines. With Lawrence, Kadeisha Buchanan, Shelina Zadorsky, Allysha Chapman, Julia Grosso, Jessie Fleming, Rebecca Quinn, and Sophie Schmidt, there's a good vibe for Canada's World Cup prospects.

KEY PLAYER STATS
(Total career goals with their country)

	Games Played	Goals
Christine Sinclair	275	178
Desiree Scott	136	0
Ashley Lawrence	69	5

WHAT TO WATCH FOR ON TV—HOW MARTA, MORGAN, HEATH, AND OTHERS PLAY

On the road to France 2019 many players helped the Canadian cause, including Christine Sinclair, Sophie Schmidt, Janine Beckie, Nichelle Prince, Jessie Fleming, Diana Matheson, Rebecca Quinn, Deanne Rose, Desiree Scott, Julia Grosso, Ashley Lawrence, Lindsay Agnew, Kadeisha Buchanan, Shelina Zadorsky, Allysha Chapman, and Stephanie Labbe in goal. During Canada's quest to World Cup glory in France, don't be surprised to see a 4-2-3-1 or possibly a 4-3-3.

Tactics and strategies: Canada must find ways to get Christine Sinclair going, use the wings as a decoy, and stay upbeat. Christine Sinclair is obviously the player Canada wants to get the most out of. Getting the ball to her feet as often as possible will only make everyone else better. That's the benefit to having a great player like Sinclair; her skill will help the flow of play, and, when she has the ball, it will attract the attention of defenders, theoretically creating opportunities for her teammates.

Canada should avoid using the predictable tactic of attacking the wings as the primary approach to its offense. Instead, it should focus attention on the "illusion" of attacking the wings but in essence the ball should be going in and out of the middle positions as often as possible. What does this really mean? Never attack down the wings? Not at all. There's nothing wrong with attacking the wings. Canada should, in fact, utilize this option throughout its games. However, and this point is very important, Canada should attempt to use the wings as a decoy. How can it do this? By playing the ball out wide often, having the outside mids dribble down the side a bit with intent, then redistributing the ball into the middle. Keep in mind, the outside mids don't always have to dribble down the side with intent, but they can always just play the ball back into the middle. Each situation is different.

When employing this tactic, Canada should also limit crossing the ball into the box. Instead, it should try to find passing combinations—coupled with thoughtful and inventive bouts of dribbling—around the box to create scoring opportunities. Crossing the ball into the box is fine, Canada should not avoid this tactic altogether, but it should definitely lesson the number of crosses it sends into the box. If its wing positions are used as decoys, interesting scoring developments around the top of the box should occur more often. Canada has had trouble in the past finding its way to a World Cup championship. So far, Canada has been unsuccessful. At some point, it must start wondering, "When are we going to win this thing?" The best remedy for such thinking is to remain upbeat. Canada's worst enemy during France 2019 might end up being negative thinking. All the Canadians have to do is take it one game at a time. Canada should also avoid thinking, "This might be Christine Sinclair's last tournament. What are we going to do after that?" Not good thoughts to have. She's here right now; go with it. Worry about her retirement and how you're going to replace her down the road. This team, ranked a respectable number 5 in the world by FIFA prior to this tournament, is one that can definitely get out of its World Cup slump from past years, and, with some good fortune, make it to the final. It's a good team coming off a second-place finish at the 2018 CONCACAF Women's Championship, with high-ranking and experienced players. Coach Kenneth Heiner-Moller and veteran Christine Sinclair have a unique opportunity to lead Canada into the history books. Landing in Group E was definitely a good start. There shouldn't be much of a problem with Cameroon, New Zealand, or the Netherlands. There could be a problem, of course, but these aren't the most dynamic teams, traditionally speaking. As far as groups go, Canada was lucky not to share one with France or Japan, for example. So most definitely Group E should provide the Canadians a window of opportunity for gaining a lot of momentum.

As Canada moves into the elimination rounds, the biggest challenge should come from the traditional powerhouses, such as Germany, Norway, and the United States, not to mention China, Japan, and Brazil. Should Canada stay organized and not get deflated with low-scoring games, then without a doubt, the sky's the limit.

Overall Team Ranking: 9.5
FIFA Ranking Going Into the World Cup: 5

CAMEROON

Twitter @FIFAWWC*
World Cup titles: 0
Africa Women's Championships: 0

Known for:
A promising program in the works
Its second World Cup appearance
Nickname: Indomitable Lionesses
Gabrielle Onguene

A BRIEF TEAM HISTORY

Basically, the women's team from Cameroon has no championships to speak of. As far as World Cups go, it didn't compete from 1991 through 2011. In World Cup 2015, which it finally qualified for, Cameroon was placed in Group C with Japan, Switzerland, and Ecuador, and eventually earned second place. From there it got to the round of 16 before losing to China 1-0.

---

*   A Twitter account for the women's national team of Cameroon could not be found. Instead, FIFA's Twitter account could possibly guide you to information about Cameroon's team.

As for the 2019 World Cup, Cameroon's second, it should be another learning experience and one to reflect on down the road as the program continues to strive for improvement. Thus far, a victory has come in the form of getting to its second World Cup. Should Cameroon advance into the elimination rounds, it will be a great achievement and something to build on for next time around.

Evidently, the women's team of Cameroon won first place at the 2011 All-Africa Games. (However, this would not be considered Africa's best tournament by most people. Hence, in the listing up top for the African Women's Championship, also known as the Africa Cup of Nations, Cameroon has zero.)

FACTS ABOUT THEIR COUNTRY

Cameroon, a West African nation, has a population of around 23 million people. Yaounde is the capital, and the country's main languages are English and French. France 2019 is the second World Cup for the women of Cameroon, otherwise known as the Indomitable Lionesses.

JOSEPH NDOKO—A BRIEF COACHING POR-TRAIT

According to FIFA, Joseph Ndoko is the coach of Cameroon leading into France 2019. The issue at hand for the coach has everything to do with leading a team ranked 46 in the world by FIFA to the final game of Cameroon's second World Cup appearance. Anything is possible, and, yes, there is potential for Cameroon to become champions in France. At best, this is a difficult task. At worst, it will be a challenge to place third in the group stage. The opposition in Cameroon's group includes Canada, New Zealand, and the Netherlands. New Zealand should be the easiest competition, but coaching-wise, Canada and the Netherlands represent a firm challenge. Like Argentina and Chile, Cameroon is a major underdog at France 2019. Getting Cameroon to this World Cup is one thing, and it was a great achievement, but navigating through the forest of ultra-talented, experienced teams *at the World Cup* is going to be the coach's biggest challenge yet.

KEY PLAYERS AND THEIR CHARACTERISTICS

Gabrielle Onguene and Madeleine Ngono Mani

Gabrielle Onguene is a forward who has recently gained experience with the club ZFK CSKA Moscow. She has over 50 caps with Cameroon and should be one of the leaders on the field.

Madeleine Ngono Mani is a proven scorer with Cameroon, and she'll be sure to keep defenses off-balance.

KEY PLAYER STATS
(Total career goals with their country)

	Games Played	Goals
Gabrielle Onguene	53	15
Madeleine Ngono Mani	76	40

WHAT TO WATCH FOR ON TV—HOW MARTA, MORGAN, HEATH, AND OTHERS PLAY

Prior to France 2019, FIFA had Cameroon ranked number 46 in the world. Not a good place to be. The tournament will be a bit challenging for the women of Cameroon. Escaping group play will be the first such challenge, and following that, should it get that far, will be higher ranked teams that are vastly more experienced at the World Cup level. A few of the players that got Cameroon to this point include Gabrielle Onguene, Madeleine Ngono Mani, Christine Manie, Claudine Meffometou, Francine Zouga, Genevieve Ngo, and Raissa Feudjio.

Tactics and strategies: Cameroon should definitely focus on counterattacking for its attack. Also, it should get numbers up, have wings join the attack, and make sure there are options around the box for potential scoring chances. Defensively, Cameroon should not get discouraged if a player gets beat on the dribble. Contain, don't lunge, and remain patient. If a player gets beat on the dribble, the response should not be trepidation for the next play. Rather, Cameroon's players should stay confident and keep this attitude going throughout an entire game, and, subsequently, the tournament.

While Cameroon is a team on the rise, it should have a major challenge this World Cup, but, nonetheless, exciting games should follow.

Overall Team Ranking: 5.4
FIFA Ranking Going Into the World Cup: 46

NEW ZEALAND

Twitter @NZ_Football
World Cup titles: 0
OFC Women's Nations Cup (previously called the OFC Women's Championship): 6

Known for:
Nickname: Football Ferns
Tom Sermanni
Ali Riley

A BRIEF TEAM HISTORY

At the 1991 World Cup, New Zealand placed last in its group. Following that, New Zealand didn't make it back to World Cup competition until 2007 when it couldn't past the group stage. As for the World Cups of 2011 and 2015: ditto.

Despite not doing well in World Cup competitions, the Football Ferns have six championships from the OFC Women's Nations Cup (previously called the OFC Women's Championship).

FACTS ABOUT THEIR COUNTRY

New Zealand—an amazingly scenic island nation located in the Pacific Ocean near the east coast of Australia—has a population of around 4.9 million people. Its main language is English, and the capital city is Wellington. As of January 2019, Ria Percival had the most caps with 135, and Amber Hearn had the most goals with 54.

TOM SERMANNI—A BRIEF COACHING POR-TRAIT

Tom Sermanni, a former midfielder and experienced coach, coached Orlando Pride before taking on the job of coaching New Zealand. He'll likely field a 4-4-2 while leading his Football Ferns, ranked 19, into France 2019. Would Sermanni's side be considered an underdog? Absolutely, yes. Sermanni will be leading a hopeful squad while relying on his experience and wise decisions to make this tournament a success.

KEY PLAYERS AND THEIR CHARACTERISTICS

Ali Riley and Ria Percival

Ali Riley, born in 1987 in Los Angeles, California, is the captain who has the responsibility to lead this squad defensively and offensively, with the hope of finally getting New Zealand to the elimination round of a World Cup. It's been tough going so far, but with Riley on the field, New Zealanders have high hopes that things in France will change. She was listed by FIFA as New

Zealand's top player, and with her experience from Chelsea F.C. Women, things are looking up for the Football Ferns.

Ria Percival, born in England, is a steady defender who leads her women's national team with caps. She is one to keep an eye on as New Zealand tries to keep its opponents off the scoreboard in order to make a historic run into the elimination rounds, a place New Zealand has yet to be.

KEY PLAYER STATS
(Total career goals with their country)

	Games Played	Goals
Ali Riley	119	1
Ria Percival	135	14

WHAT TO WATCH FOR ON TV—HOW MARTA, MORGAN, HEATH, AND OTHERS PLAY

A few of the women who got New Zealand to this place in time include Ali Riley, Ria Percival, Annalie Longo, Betsy Hassett, Katie Bowen, Grace Jale, Paige Satchell, Malia Steinmetz, Emma Rolston, Katie Rood, Sarah Gregorius, Rosie White, Anna Green, Catherine Bott, Meikayla Moore, Rebekah Stott, Sarah Morton, Elizabeth Anton, and Stephanie Skilton.

Tactics and strategies: Likely using a 4-4-2, New Zealand is going to use all of its FIFA ranking of 19 to make a big impression in France. Watch out because this might be the year the Football Ferns make it out of group play. That would be a huge accomplishment. Thus far, all tactics and strategies have come up short. In fact, not only has New Zealand never gotten out of its World Cup group, it has always finished last in its group. Frankly speaking, for New Zealand to win the World Cup in France outright, it would probably take 36 saves per half from its goalkeeper, along with a miraculous scoring binge from every other player. To remain competitive, New Zealand should be very cautious of overcommitting on tackles. The best advice for one-on-one battles is to contain, don't lunge, and remain patient. The best way to find tackles is to anticipate them. Defensively speaking, more often than not, less talented teams like New Zealand end up reacting rather than anticipating. The key is to always anticipate. Very often, if not all the time, this distinction is the difference between good and bad teams.

In terms of offense, New Zealand must avoid falling victim to rushing things around goal. The women of New Zealand need to remain calm around goal, rely on combination passing, and patiently look for opportunities to shoot. A safety outlet for New Zealand should be in the form of its outside midfielders and defenders. As an offensive progression ensues, there will be times when New Zealand's players might get rattled by defensive pressure. During these moments, it's very easy for players to panic and force things downfield. The best option for rattled performers is to play the ball out wide and use these positions as a wall, so to speak. Working the ball off the outside players reestablishes possession, and it can alleviate pressure. Also, New Zealand must use defenders as a good way to regroup. There's nothing wrong with going backwards. In fact, it usually leads to a better option going forward a few moments later.

The coach's role in this endeavor is very important. If things aren't going well for New Zealand, should the players be spoken to with reproach? To the contrary. They should be uplifted. Sure, New Zealand has had less than spectacular results from previous World Cups. Sure, New Zealand is from the weakest confederation in the world. Sure, New Zealand wasn't ranked in the top 10 prior to this tournament. But they shouldn't be looked down on. Rather, the coach needs to convey confidence and work with the players to create a union. Furthermore, great players need to stand up and motivate their teammates. Excellent players always strive to win. As Jeff Van Gundy—a legendary basketball coach, teacher, and TV commentator—would say (paraphrasing), "Great players win." Van Gundy's words are true across the board, regardless the sport. New Zealand's great players definitely need to be "great" and start winning. The players within the locker room of New Zealand need to stand up and accept the role of being a championship-ready team.* These players have to realize that there is no better time and opportunity than a World Cup to prove this point. With the support of the coach in this regard, New Zealand is a team with boundless potential.

A major achievement for New Zealand would be to leave France having gotten to the second round. In doing so it would break this curse of the group stage from previous World Cups and set the program in a new direction. Considering New Zealand's situation, it will be a very fun team to watch.

Overall Team Ranking: 8.1
FIFA Ranking Going Into the World Cup: 19

---

* Van Gundy was preaching these very points during an *ESPN* broadcast of an NBA game between the Indiana Pacers and Washington Wizards, on January 30, 2019.

THE NETHERLANDS

Twitter @FIFAWWC*
World Cup titles: 0
European Championships: 1

Known for:
Winning the 2017 UEFA Women's Euro
Sarina Wiegman
Lieke Martens

A BRIEF TEAM HISTORY

As if awoken from a long sleep in the world of women's soccer, the Netherlands's only World Cup foray to this point was in 2015 when it got to the round of 16. France 2019 is the program's second attempt, and, for sure, the Dutch are looking to make it a memorable one.

---

* A Twitter account for the Netherlands women's national team could not be found. Instead, FIFA's Twitter account could possibly guide you to information about the team.

Indeed, it may come as a surprise to some, the Netherlands won the UEFA Women's Euro in 2017—a major feather in its hat. The Netherlands also won the 2018 Algarve Cup.

Perhaps the Dutch women have a poor World Cup record, but these two recent championships should guide the team forward with a lot of momentum, experience, and confidence into France 2019.

FACTS ABOUT THEIR COUNTRY

The Netherlands has a population of around 17 million people. Its capital city is Amsterdam. In terms of soccer, the Netherlands might as well be known as the passing capital of the world; Dutch coaching methods are renowned for their strict attention to passing and all the ways it can be perfected and improved upon after that.

SARINA WIEGMAN—A BRIEF COACHING PORTRAIT

Sarina Wiegman, born in 1969, is a former player with North Carolina University and the Dutch national team, so right off she's headed in the right direction. How can the Netherlands miss? Sarina will probably utilize a 4-3-3 in an all-out attempt at closing the deal on a World Cup championship in France, which her team—ranked number 7 in the world by FIFA prior to the tournament—is very capable of.

KEY PLAYERS AND THEIR CHARACTERISTICS

Lieke Martens, Danielle van de Donk, Sherida Spitse, and Kika van Es

Lieke Martens, who currently plays with FC Barcelona Femeni, is a salient performer for the Dutch and sure to be a focal point of opposing defenses. Martens, who FIFA listed as the Netherlands's top player going into France 2019, is a capable scorer. The 5'7" star will be doing all she can to cause havoc around her opponent's goal.

Danielle van de Donk, born in 1991, is a skillful midfielder who will keep the Netherlands in games with distribution of the ball to key parts of the field. She's been a key player with Arsenal W.F.C. and will have this valuable experience to help guide the Dutch toward a successful campaign in France.

Sherida Spitse is a midfielder with scoring capability, which is always an added bonus, and she'll be a handful for opposing teams. She's got over 150 games under her belt with the Netherlands and should be a strong asset moving forward.

Kika van Es, born in 1991, is a defender navigating the outside, keeping opposing forwards off their game.

KEY PLAYER STATS

(Total career goals with their country)

	Games Played	Goals
Lieke Martens	95	39
Danielle van de Donk	82	12
Sherida Spitse	154	29
Kika van Es	50	0

WHAT TO WATCH FOR ON TV—HOW MARTA, MORGAN, HEATH, AND OTHERS PLAY

A few players who have gotten the Netherlands to this place include Lieke Martens, Vivianne Miedema (a prolific scorer sure to keep defenses busy), Danielle van de Donk, Sherida Spitse, Desiree van Lunteren, Kika van Es, Siri Worm, Merel van Dongen, Danique Kerkdijk, Dominique Bloodworth, Liza van der Most, Kelly Zeeman, Anouk Dekker, Jill Roord, Jackie Groenen, Shanice van de Sanden, Renate Jansen, Ellen Jansen, and Lineth Beerensteyn.

Tactics and strategies: The Dutch will likely go with a 4-3-3 with Shanice van de Sanden, Vivianne Miedema, and Lieke Martens acting as the focal point up top. There's a lot of help behind them, from Sherida Spitse and others, as the Netherlands will methodically work the ball forward. A few keys to success include a strong work rate, passing combinations, and team defense. The Dutch need to bring a strong work rate to each game and outwork its opponent. In doing so, it will be able to achieve a level of superiority with its passing game. The Netherlands represents the land of brilliant passers. As a team, the Dutch need to overwhelm opponents with high-quality combination passing. It needs to work the ball across the field, with forwards checking in and out, and then openings will gradually emerge in the opposition's defensive areas. Should the Dutch out-pass its opponents, long-term success should arise. The Dutch have to stay focused on defense and act as one unit. In doing so, each player needs to look for deflections in order to cause turnovers, which will lead to transition play. If the Netherlands remains strong as a solidified unit on defense, these little nuances should occur in its favor. At that point, the Netherlands should have an advantage over its opponents.

Another simple idea the Netherlands should keep in mind is trying shots from distance and following up for rebounds. The Dutch have an opportunity in France to outthink its opponents, outplay its opponents, and out-pass its opponents. On top of this, the Netherlands should look to hit shots from distance, and distance in this case is referring to around 18 yards outside the goal. A neighbor of the Dutch, a longtime player and coach, Franz Beckenbauer, often has favored trying shots from this area occasionally. Some people tend to shy away from this line of thinking. In the case of the Dutch, why not? Give it a go and have a few shots from outside the box. See what happens. But don't make this the main focus of the attack. Instead, the Netherlands should use this tactic sporadically.

It's a team that was ranked number 7 in the world leading into this tournament, and, with a little luck here and there, it should have a strong presence in France 2019 and in more competitions down the road.

Overall Team Ranking: 9.3
FIFA Ranking Going Into the World Cup: 7

THAILAND

Twitter @FIFAWWC*
World Cup titles: 0
AFC Women's Asian Cup: 1

Known for:
Winning the 1983 AFC Women's Championship (the AFC Women's Asian Cup)
A soccer program on the move
Duangnapa Sritala
Kanjana Sungngoen

A BRIEF TEAM HISTORY

Thailand's first World Cup appearance was in 2015, but it didn't get past the group stage. Now it's back for the 2019 World Cup in France, looking to improve drastically.

---

* A Twitter account for the women's national team of Thailand could not be found. Instead, FIFA's Twitter account could possibly guide you to information about Thailand's team.

To its credit, Thailand won the 1983 AFC Women's Championship. Thailand has also won the AFF Women's Championship in 2011, 2015, 2016, and 2018. The AFF (ASEAN Football Federation) Women's Championship features teams from Southeast Asia. It's a less prestigious tournament, which is why Thailand was given only one score for Asian Championships in the opening credits.

FACTS ABOUT THEIR COUNTRY

Thailand is a beautiful country in Southeast Asia known for its amazing cuisine, one that features elaborate curry dishes, including that of green, red, and yellow. Oddly enough, of the curries, yellow is the only one that universally goes well with potatoes (of course, this is a personal preference, but, nonetheless, it's an opinion pretty much accepted across the board). The capital of Thailand is Bangkok, which is also its most well-known city, and, not to mention, of all the cities throughout greater Thailand, it has the largest population. The overall population of Thailand is around 68.8 million people. One of the nation's most popular beers is Singha, which is sure to be passed around as fans watch the women's team compete in France.

NUENGRUETHAI SATHONGWIEN—A BRIEF COACHING PORTRAIT

Under coach Nuengruethai Sathongwien, Thailand will probably go with a 4-4-2. For coach Sathongwien, France 2019 could be a surprising fairy tale tournament for Thailand or a complete disaster. It will be a challenge for sure, as Thailand begins play in a group with Sweden, Chile, and the United States. Not much is expected of Thailand, but coach Sathongwien will want to keep scores low and concentrate on the fairy tale aspect of things.

KEY PLAYERS AND THEIR CHARACTERISTICS

Silawan Intamee, Duangnapa Sritala, and Kanjana Sungngoen

Silawan Intamee, born in 1994, will be guiding things from the midfield, distributing the ball and hoping to link up with teammates in an effort to create a few upsets in France 2019.

Duangnapa Sritala, born in 1986, is a defender and leader for Thailand. She'll be responsible for the monumental task of getting Thailand out of its group, which will be a challenge, to say the least.

Kanjana Sungngoen was listed by FIFA as Thailand's top player going into the 2019 World Cup. She's a goal-scorer with at least 30 goals for her country, and she's looking to add more. Keep an eye on her as Thailand figures out its group. She'll be vital for success, and Thailand is counting on her for goals, and plenty of them.

KEY PLAYER STATS
(Total career goals with their country)

	Games Played	Goals
Silawan Intamee	14	0
Duangnapa Sritala	25	2
Kanjana Sungngoen	47	30

WHAT TO WATCH FOR ON TV—HOW MARTA, MORGAN, HEATH, AND OTHERS PLAY

Silawan Intamee, Sunisa Srangthaisong, Suchawadee Nildhamrong, Natthakarn Chinwong, Duangnapa Sritala, Ainon Phancha, Warunee Phetwiset, Pikul Khueanpet, Orathai Srimanee, Alisa Rukpinij, Rattikan Thongsombut, Taneekarn Dangda, Kanjana Sungngoen, and Khwanrudi Saengchan are a few players who placed Thailand in a position to succeed in France 2019.

Can Thailand—which will probably go with a 4-4-2—win the World Cup? Can Thailand succeed in France 2019? Yes and maybe. Yes, in that it's possible, though highly unlikely. Maybe, in that success for Thailand will be of a lower bar. For sure, it's a team with less experience that some of the giants of the tournament. For sure, it's a team that has very little experience at the World Cup level. With this in mind, success for Thailand will be getting out of its group and taking things one step at a time. That is, should Thailand get out of its group. At best, this will be a difficult task. At worst, it should be surprising if Thailand scores a goal. Keep in mind, a few years back, in 2016, Thailand lost a friendly match to the United States by a score of 9-0.

Tactics and strategies: Thailand must stay united as a team, not lose focus, and establish passing connections. It's in Thailand's best interest to stay united as a group. The scores might get out of hand. The last thing Thailand needs is for players to begin bickering on the field; this usually leads to worse results.

Thailand needs to concentrate on small battles around the field. It needs to forget about the big picture stuff. The grand stage of the World Cup is too big for a newcomer like Thailand to get wrapped up in. Each player needs to establish small battles with the opposition and focus on tackles, loose balls, and intercepting passes. All these little defensive things can potentially add up in Thailand's favor. In doing so, the Thai players need to "let the offense come to them." It's something said often by coaches, and it couldn't be more true. This is key. Let good defense be the offense. This should be the main focus for the team.

Also, after Thailand has established some confidence in its defensive stance, it needs to look for passing connections, even if the passing connections lead to nowhere. This doesn't matter. Eventually nowhere passes lead to something brilliant. It's just a matter of time. In this respect, Thailand needs to be patient in the passing game. Rushing things will not be in Thailand's best interest whatsoever. Which players need to set the tone for patience in passing? Quite specifically, the backline and center mids. Everything starts with the backline; in other words, each and every offensive attack likely has something to do with the defenders. In general, defenders get the most touches and start almost every offensive attack, so therefore it is absolutely imperative for Thailand's defenders to take responsibility for guiding the initial passing connections that will galvanize the possession game. The defenders have to incorporate the center mids in this effort, as the center mids are very valuable.

Thailand has a women's program that is gaining a foothold in international soccer, and this World Cup in France should be pivotal for experience to build on down the road.

Overall Team Ranking: 7.1
FIFA Ranking Going Into the World Cup: 29

CHILE

Twitter @FIFAWWC*
World Cup titles: 0
South American Championships: 0

Known for:
Jose Letelier
Christiane Endler

A BRIEF TEAM HISTORY

Some teams rule the World Cup—the United States, Germany. Other teams make a big splash—Norway, Japan. Other teams do very well—Brazil, Sweden, China. Then other teams show up for the first time. That would be Chile. For the women on Chile's team, this is the inaugural tournament in a World Cup; it's the *inaugural* showing, though Chile is hoping for many more down the line. Regardless how well Chile ends up doing, it's a team and country that has made history already. With that said, each game

---

* A Twitter account for the women's national team of Chile could not be found. Instead, FIFA's Twitter account could possibly guide you to information about Chile's team.

for Chile should be interesting, and with each performance there will possibly be a sign of things to come in the near future.

FACTS ABOUT THEIR COUNTRY

Chile, which makes up a thin strip of land on the west coast of South America, has approximately 17.5 million people, and its capital is Santiago.

JOSE LETELIER—A BRIEF COACHING POR-TRAIT

Jose Letelier, born in 1966 in Santiago, Chile, will probably utilize a 4-4-2 on his quest for greatness in France. Letelier, a former goalie, is leading a Chilean side that was ranked number 38 in the world by FIFA prior to this tournament. Given that his team has little shot to win the World Cup outright, he has room to experiment with lineups and possibly give some subs an experience-building opportunity at the World Cup level. Letelier's dream would be to surpass all expectations and make history by winning the whole thing, which, in fact, would make history and then some. However, any coach in his position has to be a realist on some level, and building on this outing for future generations of Chilean players is the best bet right now.

KEY PLAYERS AND THEIR CHARACTERISTICS

Christiane Endler, Yessenia Lopez, and Su Helen Galaz

Chile's goalkeeper Christiane Endler—born in 1991, standing at around 5'11"—was listed by FIFA as Chile's top player going into France 2019. This might seem odd to some people for one simple reason: Quite often a goalkeeper is not considered a team's top player. Of course, great goalies are highly regarded, but they usually aren't given such an honor before field players, so, in fact, Endler must be feeling pretty good about it, and, to be sure, her teammates are certainly calmer knowing they have a stellar keeper in front of the net.

Yessenia Lopez, born in 1990 in Vina del Mar, Chile, will be found in midfield leading the cause for Chile with passing and a creative touch around goal.

Su Helen Galaz is a defender who has made her way to Zaragoza CFF, a club team in Spain. She'll be a vital component with her teammates on defense to help Christiane Endler keep a clean sheet.

KEY PLAYER STATS
(Total career goals with their country)

	Games Played	Goals
Christiane Endler	17	0
Yessenia Lopez	13	3
Su Helen Galaz	9	0

WHAT TO WATCH FOR ON TV—HOW MARTA, MORGAN, HEATH, AND OTHERS PLAY

While Christiane Endler is keeping the goal safe, her teammates—Maria Jose Rojas at forward, Yessenia Lopez in the midfield, Su Helen Galaz on defense, along with the supporting cast—will be doing what they can to pull off a first-time World Cup fairy tale story en route to the championship game. While this might be highly unlikely, it's worth a try, and each game represents the unthinkable opportunity for Chile to be that fairy tale team. Standing behind what will likely be a 4-4-2, Endler will be called upon to protect the goal with everything she's got. Should the defense hold up, Endler's goalkeeping skills, which are highly thought of, should keep the scores low for the Chileans. That is to say, if the defense can hold up. Sometimes if a team becomes too unorganized, the floodgates can open up, and whether there's a good goalie or not, the score can get out of control.

Tactics and strategies: Chile will likely rely on defensive prowess while utilizing a counterattack to its advantage, and a lot of it. A good defense might just be Chile's best offensive weapon. As it sits back, which it will (considering it's a new team to the World Cup), Chile should unleash multiple counterattacks throughout each game. It will need the base of its defense to be strong, and this should allow for offensive movement afterward. The counterattack will be its best avenue of attack. After Chile produces a counter, it has to be mindful of transition play the other way and get back into defensive shape to prevent a good scoring chance from its opposition. It's common-sense soccer, but, at the World Cup level, a grand stage that Chile is very unfamiliar with, things might get out of control, and its players need to remember the absolute basics.

Psychologically speaking, since this is Chile's first World Cup, it needs to think defense first. However, only thinking defensively will be a recipe for disaster. Somehow, Chile's coach, Letelier, must instill in his players the core belief of defense first and gradual offense from there. Offensive production might come in intermittent spurts, and there's nothing wrong with that, but, collectively as a team, Chile needs to understand this. It needs to accept the fact that it might not be the best outing. But, for things to potentially go in Chile's favor, the players need to understand the balance between defense first and offense second.

The keys on defense for Chile include anticipation, one-on-one defending, and anticipation. Anticipation is so important for any team, especially one embarking on its debut World Cup appearance. Inexperienced teams tend to react to an offensive buildup; these teams will sit back and wait and wait and wait, and then react to a play made. Instead, inexperienced players need to anticipate a play. Reacting to a play leaves players in no-man's-land. Anticipating a play tends to break up the play in question. The latter is good. The former is not so good. If players are reacting, then, in essence, they're simply allowing the other team to do whatever they want. Then a reaction occurs because the less experienced team thinks an appropriate moment has occurred to break up a play. Rather, anticipation is telling the opposing offense that you know what they're doing. You're not reacting to a play, as if you need permission, you're anticipating, and, in effect, you're outthinking the opponent (by letting them know that you know what they're doing). Chile needs to be assertive in this regard and anticipate plays, instead of becoming victim to such a thing.

One-on-one defense requires much of the same attention to anticipation. Chile should not lunge or jump in or overreact.

Rather, Chile needs to stay consistent in its approach with one-on-one defense, and make sure that each player is constantly alert and ready to double-team with defensive support. And finally, back to anticipation again. Chile must focus its attention on the need for anticipation and not reaction. Distinguishing between the two is crucial, and for any success in France, the Chilean players must be thinking together in order to outfox the opposition with anticipation.

Realistically, what are Chile's chances of winning the World Cup? How does one go about explaining this? Not very good. Is there hope? Sure, but not much. Chile has a long road to travel in order to become a top-tier program. This is its first World Cup appearance for the women, and, who knows, it might be the last. For the sake of Chile's progression in international soccer, an experience like this one is placing Chile's soccer program on the right track for future success. Actually, there is plenty of success that Chile can find in France 2019, and that will come in the form of little victories throughout the tournament. But for Chile to have big victories, in the form of getting to the quarterfinals or even the championship game, it needs to regroup after this tournament, access the damage, and improve things from there. After all, there is no reason why Chile cannot become a world power. Regardless, Chile will be an interesting team to watch.

Overall Team Ranking: 6.2
FIFA Ranking Going Into the World Cup: 38

SWEDEN

Twitter @FIFAWWC*
World Cup titles: 0
European Championships: 1

Known for:
Exciting games
Therese Sjogran
Lotta Schelin
Linda Sembrant
Kosovare Asllani
Caroline Seger
Sofia Jakobsson
Stina Blackstenius

A BRIEF TEAM HISTORY

Where it matters, the World Cup, Sweden has done fairly well over the years. Right out of the gates, at the 1991 World Cup

---

* A Twitter account for the women's national team of Sweden could not be found. Instead, FIFA's Twitter account could possibly guide you to information about Sweden's team.

in China, Sweden placed third overall. At the following World Cup, which it hosted in 1995, Sweden wasn't so fortunate, losing in the quarterfinals. At the 1999 World Cup in the United States, Sweden would again lose in the quarterfinals. It was supposed to be up and away from third place and into the final match…didn't quite happen. Two consecutive World Cup losses in the quarterfinals were getting in the way of a bigger dream.

World Cup 2003 was a different story for the talented Swedes who started out by placing second in Group A, right behind the United States and in front of North Korea and Nigeria. Sweden took it to Brazil in the quarterfinals, winning 2-1, and, in the semi-finals, the Swedes got the same score against Canada, setting up for a showdown in the final with Germany. Though it wouldn't be Sweden's tournament as it lost by the familiar score of 2-1 and had to watch on as its historic rival Germany lifted the grand trophy for the first time.

While the 2003 World Cup was so close for the Swedes, the Cup was a bust in 2007 as Sweden couldn't get out of Group B, which contained the United States, North Korea, and Nigeria. World Cup 2011 was a turnaround year as Sweden improved drastically, eventually taking third place. Then 2015 came around, and it was back to average as the Swedes lost in the round of 16 to Germany. Always a competitive team, it's one that is seeking that elusive world championship. And Sweden has some swagger going into France 2019; this might be the year.

Aside from flirtatious moments with the World Cup, Sweden has, in fact, conquered Europe on at least one occasion when it won the 1984 European Competition for Women's Football (now called the UEFA Women's Euro). Sweden has also won the Algarve Cup four times in 1995, 2001, 2009, and 2018.

FACTS ABOUT THEIR COUNTRY

Sweden's population of around 10.2 million people is governed from the capital of Stockholm. For beer, Swedes have a few domestic breweries to choose from, including Spendrups and Kronleins. Therese Sjogran has the most caps for the Swedish women's national team, with 214. Sweden's top scorer is Lotta Schelin, with 88 goals.

PETER GERHARDSSON—A BRIEF COACHING PORTRAIT

Peter Gerhardsson, born in 1959, is a former forward with an offensive eye for a strong Swedish side ready for big results in France 2019. On his quest for the cup, Gerhardsson might go with a 3-4-1-2 or a 4-2-3-1, with a flurry of attackers at his ready, including Kosovare Asllani, Caroline Seger, Sofia Jakobsson, and Stina Blackstenius.

KEY PLAYERS AND THEIR CHARACTERISTICS

Linda Sembrant, Kosovare Asllani, Caroline Seger, Stina Blackstenius, and Sofia Jakobsson

Linda Sembrant, born in 1987 in Uppsala, Sweden, is a defender with experience from Montpellier in France, among other clubs.

She's a veteran with Sweden expected to keep things in order on the backline. She's not a huge scorer but has been known to put the ball in the back of the net from time to time; as a center defender, overlooking the development of the attack, she'll be vital in Sweden's all-around progression throughout France 2019.

Kosovare Asllani, born in 1989 in Kristianstad, Sweden, is a very experienced player with Sweden's national team who got her start back in 2008. She also has a multitiered résumé of club teams, including Manchester City and Paris Saint-Germain. She'll use her craft and guile in the midfield to open up opportunities for herself and teammates as Sweden makes a strong surge toward the final.

Caroline Seger, the all-around talent, the leader of the team, the captain, has experience with a number of clubs, including a brief tour with Philadelphia Independence a few years back. Seger is the heartbeat of the team, conducting things generally from center midfield with a hand in offense and defense. She has a vast amount of experience, which should serve Sweden well throughout the tournament. This might be the last World Cup for Seger, and to capture Sweden's first title on this stage would be a dream come true.

Stina Blackstenius was listed by FIFA as Sweden's top player prior to France 2019. She can be found up top creating scoring opportunities as part of a talented and lethal offensive combination. Born in 1996, Stina is one of the younger players on board, but she's still being counted on for big results.

Sofia Jakobsson is a forward with experience at Montpellier among other clubs; she's one of Sweden's leading attackers and sure to keep opposing teams off-balance.

KEY PLAYER STATS

(Total career goals with their country)

	Games Played	Goals
Linda Sembrant	102	8
Kosovare Asllani	120	31
Caroline Seger	186	26
Stina Blackstenius	40	10
Sofia Jakobsson	93	15

WHAT TO WATCH FOR ON TV—HOW MARTA, MORGAN, HEATH, AND OTHERS PLAY

Sweden is going to produce a very determined and aggressive side eager for a championship. It has come so close in the past, and as the years tick by, the Swedes are looking to grab a hold of the most coveted trophy.

Tactics and strategies: From the beginning to the end of the tournament, Sweden needs to establish quick distribution of the ball out to the wings in order to generate passing connections, offensive flow, and rhythm. It must do this by having its center mids actively seeking out such opportunities. Playing the ball out wide will play to Sweden's strengths, which involve getting the ball from wide positions into the box for strong scoring chances. Sweden is very capable of dominating with this approach, and it should have success if done correctly.

The Swedes aren't necessarily going to dazzle any opponents with the skill seen from Brazilian and American players, such as Marta and Tobin Heath. However, Sweden may have a few tricks up its sleeve. The question of how many tricks is debatable, but expect to see more of an established, organized attack with momentum coming from outside overlapping support. There should likely be a lot of balls played into the box for target players Stina Blackstenius and Sofia Jakobsson, while Kosovare Asllani and Caroline Seger provide organizational support from midfield. Sweden's team is full of talent. At any moment the scoring could open up for Sweden as it's looking to blow teams out of the water. Defensively, Sweden should concentrate on a zone deep within its own half while being mindful of runners that will lead to one-on-one marking to avoid immediate threats.

In the buildup to France 2019, FIFA had Sweden ranked at number 9 in the world, which is a great place to be if you're Sweden. It's a top 10 ranking, which provides the team confidence, yet it's far enough away from the top position to motivate the players to a higher level. Linda Sembrant, Kosovare Asllani, Caroline Seger, Stina Blackstenius, and Sofia Jakobsson should definitely help lead this cause, and, when it's all said and done, they might go down in history as leaders of an elite Swedish side.

Overall Team Ranking: 9.1
FIFA Ranking Going Into the World Cup: 9

THE STADIUMS OF
FRANCE 2019

Games for the 2019 FIFA Women's World Cup will take place in Lyon, Paris, Nice, Montpellier, Rennes, Le Havre, Valenciennes, Reims, and Grenoble.

LYON, FRANCE

Stadium: Parc Olympique Lyonnais

With room for just over 59,000, Parc Olympique Lyonnais is the largest venue for the 2019 Women's World Cup. Lyon, located in the central-eastern part of France, will be a phenomenal setting for large crowds and historic World Cup excitement.

PARIS, FRANCE

Stadium: Parc des Princes

With room for over 48,000 fans, Parc des Princes will be rocking with action for games in the notorious, beautiful, historic, classy, artistic, romantic, and ever-exciting Paris.

NICE, FRANCE

Stadium: Allianz Riviera

Located down in the beautiful southwestern part of France, Allianz Riviera seats over 35,000 people, and this should be an ideal setting for World Cup action. The streets of Nice should be full of parties at night.

MONTPELLIER, FRANCE

Stadium: Stade de la Mosson

With a capacity of close to 33,000, Stade de la Mosson is an ideal setting for soccer fans visiting the astounding south of France (very close to Spain), along with all the Mediterranean culture of Montpellier. The local restaurant scene will provide interesting options for World Cup tourists visiting for the first time.

RENNES, FRANCE

Stadium: Roazhon Park

With room for a little over 29,000 people, Roazhon Park is situated in the gorgeous landscape of northwestern France. Amazing wine, beer, and local food will be on display for fans.

LE HAVRE, FRANCE

Stadium: Stade Oceane

Stade Oceane seats a little over 25,000 fans, and it's situated in the scenic northern part of France, facing the English Channel. With a little motivation, fans might hop over to England for a quick drink or two.

VALENCIENNES, FRANCE

Stadium: Stade du Hainaut

With a little over 25,000 capacity, this exquisite stadium rests in northern France, relatively close to Le Havre, Paris, and Reims.

It's a great region for travelers to experience the World Cup and explore France.

REIMS, FRANCE

Stadium: Stade Auguste-Delaune

This marvelous stadium has space for approximately 21,000 people, and it rests in lovely northeastern France, near Paris. Fans can take a quick trip to Paris or enjoy the active World Cup nightlife of Reims.

GRENOBLE, FRANCE

Stadium: Stade des Alpes

This is a beautiful stadium located in the southeast of France with room for a little over 20,000. Outside the stadium, World Cup fans will have the brilliant options of local wine and cuisine.

Geographically speaking, France is a relatively small country, and it should be quite easy for fans to travel from city to city by car, train, or possibly bus (the train system in France is particularly good). You can't rule out helicopter travel either.

Travel around France will certainly be better than it was for fans attending the World Cup 2015 in Canada. In Canada, for example, the games were hosted in the following cities (from east to west): Moncton, Montreal, Ottawa, Winnipeg, Edmonton, and Vancouver. That's a vast distance to travel, and, it should go without saying, a little impractical by car, and even by air unless the travelers in question were very motivated. If such travel occurred, if fans drove from city to city to view games, a proper title of "Super Fan" should be appointed, along with special T-shirts to commemorate the accomplishment, followed by a series of calls to the *Guinness Book of World Records* on their behalf. The proximity of cities within France makes it an ideal location for this grand event. Fans will be able to enjoy as much of the action as possible while also sneaking in a winery visit or two.

As France eventually was granted the honor of hosting the World Cup, the bidding started back in 2014. Other countries with bids to host included South Korea, South Africa, England, and New Zealand. Subsequently, when it was announced by FIFA that France would be the location for the 2019 Women's World Cup, it established the first time the French would host the event. Previously, France had hosted the men's World Cup in the years of 1938 and 1998. Now, as a soccer-hosting nation, France can claim both honors.

Furthermore, in 1998, the French men won the title. Much of France's success in 1998 had to do with a player named Zinedine Zidane and also the power of the home crowd. The latter is a very important factor, and it has guided multiple teams to titles over the years, whether it be the men's or women's World Cup. For a championship run in 2019, the French women are hoping to acquire some of the home crowd magic the French men had in 1998, which, if the women can pull it off, would be France's first World Cup title on the women's side.

WOMEN'S WORLD
CUP HISTORY

Past Winners
- 1991: United States
- 1995: Norway
- 1999: United States
- 2003: Germany
- 2007: Germany
- 2011: Japan
- 2015: United States

In 1991, the Women's World Cup was held in China. While the United States women took home the first trophy, Norway came in second with Sweden following in third, and Germany in fourth. It was a great start for the US women, a trend that would continue.

The Women's World Cup of 1995 was hosted in the great northern country of Sweden. Swedish neighbor Norway took home the first-place prize, with Germany placing second while the United States got third, and China finished in fourth.

The Women's 1999 World Cup took place in the United States with a remarkable turnout. Soccer in the United States—with many thanks to the women's side—was taking off with amazing excitement. Coached by Tony DiCicco, the US fielded probably its best team in women's soccer history, featuring the likes of Mia Hamm, Julie Foudy, Kristine Lilly, Cindy Parlow, Tiffeny Milbrett, the brilliant Michelle Akers, Joy Fawcett, Carla Overbeck, the speedy Kate Sobrero, Shannon MacMillan, Tisha Venturini, Sara Whalen, and Briana Scurry in goal. There was practically nothing more exciting in 1999 than Brandi Chastain knocking home the winning kick in a penalty shootout against China in a packed Rose Bowl Stadium. The crowd seemed to crackle when cheers erupted as the women stormed the field in celebration. China had an extremely talented passing team that year and deservedly made the finals. It was only fitting that both teams would have to decide the game over penalty kicks. The third-place finisher of 1999 was Brazil, and Norway took home fourth.

In 2003, the United States hosted again, but, unfortunately for the Americans, Germany took home the title, with Sweden taking second, the US in third, and Canada earning a fourth-place finish. The 2007 World Cup was featured in China as Germany took home the championship for the second time in a row. Brazil finished second, the US took third, while Norway got in the books with a fourth-place finish. The 2011 World Cup took place in beautiful Germany. The Germans didn't win a third title in a row. In fact, Germany didn't make the top four. First place went to Japan, the first Asian team to win the Women's World Cup. The US came in second, Sweden finished third, and France took fourth. The most recent World Cup of 2015 flourished in Canada. For the US, it was a great opportunity to regain its place as the world's number one.

For the US, taking home the title was a huge relief. The second-place finish went to Japan. England got on the board with a third-place finish, and Germany landed in fourth. The following are updated blog entries from World Cup 2015, which, in part, were published online at Cardinal Publishers Group in June 2015.

THE 2015 WOMEN'S WORLD CUP
US VS. AUSTRALIA
GROUP PLAY
3-1

In every World Cup, the US women are the favorites. Though most would have agreed that the Germans appeared to be the forerunners this time around. Julie Foudy, a graduate of Stanford University and a member of the women's 1999 championship side, was one to point out the artificial turf being a ridiculous choice for a tournament such as this. Regardless, both teams have to play on it, as they say.

Going into the first match for the US, it was not expected to be a walk in the park as the Australian bunch—known in some circles as the "Matildas"—had managed to stay competitive over the years. The team Australia fielded in the previous World Cup had some time and experience for reflection. The young Australian players, including Kyah Simon and Caitlin Foord, had the responsibility to lead the team this time around.

For the US, Carli Lloyd, alongside an injured Alex Morgan, would be leading the cause. Carli Lloyd, thought by some to be the best midfielder of her generation, is a good player but not quite the caliber of Aly Wagner or Michelle Akers of years past, who many feel represent the ceiling for quality midfield play, both in skill and technique, combined with that innate ability to create chances that others simply do not see.

The Australian side gave the US a good run but fell short of walking away with a key win. The US started out slow and very impatiently. The keeper, Hope Solo, had to make a number of saves in the first half. Add to that, with little buildup in possession from the back, the US looked like it was trying to get things arranged but couldn't quite find the right path. While in the second half, the team picked up the pace and the play became crisper, with energy brought from the bench. The buildup from the back improved, and the first game ended in a 3-1 victory.

With steady keeper play, the team got the jitters out, and moved onward to the next step. Possibly, with Morgan's injury, the team needed to find a way to keep things moving in a positive direction toward the next challenge.

THE 2015 WOMEN'S WORLD CUP
US VS. SWEDEN
GROUP PLAY
0-0

Even though it turned out to be a tie, the US women looked much better in this second game against Sweden. That is, in the *second half* of this second game. Despite strong defense from the US in the first 45, the front side of the attack was lacking a connection as opportunities in the box were missed, with a through pass massively over-paced as the first half came to a close, thus missing out on a prime opportunity to create danger in Sweden's box.

As the team regrouped at half, the pace in the next 45 was much better. As the Winnipeg-based crowd lifted the spirits of the players, there was good patience in possession, the spacing was exploited in Sweden's defensive third, along with good footwork from Lloyd and Krieger; Christen Press was very composed. Lloyd came very close to scoring near the Swede's goal line, which turned into a clash of heads, leaving both players on the ground momentarily. There was a close call for a penalty kick as the ball ambiguously glazed off a Swedish defender's hand, but the real attacking threat came from a delicate shot past Solo which a US defender deflected off her head into the crossbar, averting a near certain score from Sweden.

In the end, a 0-0 score would be the result, as the US moved on with a point, now at the top of Group D with four points.

THE 2015 WOMEN'S WORLD CUP
US VS. NIGERIA
GROUP PLAY
1-0

Wambach's goal, a volley with her foot—not her head—put the US past Nigeria, as predicted (by most) to win Group D. The midfield was better, with room for improvement. This win avoided a second-round game against a strong Brazilian side. After coming off a tie against Sweden, this was a great confidence builder for the team during the next few days. Considering the point structure within group play, a tie leaves players to wonder. Furthermore, Morgan's start was the first in two months, due to an injury comeback. US fans were hoping to see more from her. Combined with Lloyd, and other midfield talent, things were coming together for the US, as the team was gaining momentum heading into the knockout rounds. Some keys moving on involved the US remaining composed in possession and not getting rattled when it didn't score right away. One focal point would be a solid and relaxed defense, which, up to this point, had played well, keeping the US in games, but it had also looked jittery at times.

THE 2015 WOMEN'S WORLD CUP
US VS. COLOMBIA
SECOND ROUND
2-0

The US won 2-0 and got past Colombia as expected, but as the team prepared for a strong Chinese side, there were still questions. Julie Foudy, speaking on the *ESPN Freddie Coleman Show* said, "Get stuck in," with a laugh, responding to his question on how the US could defeat China in the quarterfinal match. The echo chamber was more or less: "There needs to be more cohesive play; there needs to be more aggressive tackling; better chemistry; more offense." All this was true as the squad was not playing the best soccer, but it moved on. In similar fashion to the men's Brazilian team in 2014, the US was getting by; however, the play wasn't very eye pleasing. The problem was, on paper, the team had great talent. There were moments when the talent in question was clearly on display. The players had the skill and commitment, but there was a quality lacking that was holding the players back from really getting things into high gear.

There was a lot of pressure on the team, particularly with the showdown against China...the rematch of 1999, when the best team in US women's history, led by Akers and Hamm, was full throttle. Sometimes, with so much pressure coming from all angles, it's difficult for players to keep focused and remember the little things while playing in a game. Could the US pull it together? Could the team get past China?

THE 2015 WOMEN'S WORLD CUP
US VS. CHINA
QUARTERFINALS
1-0

"In three short weeks it has become the hottest story of the summer," said Robin Roberts from a sold-out Rose Bowl stadium in 1999. Four fighter jets soared over the crowd as the national anthem finished, and the crowd went crazy. Brandi Chastain, Kate Sobrero, Joy Fawcett, Kristine Lilly, Michelle Akers, Julie Foudy, Mia Hamm, Tiffeny Milbrett, and Cindy Parlow, to name a few. Some team.

The 2015 Women's World Cup quarterfinal between the US and China was said to be a "rematch" of sorts. The US women had a lot to live up to. The team wasn't just playing in a rematch against China from 1999, but it was also playing against the US team of 1999, so to speak, trying to live up to that epic standard. Everything was on the line for the US in 2015, including its reputation and a place in the semi-finals. The US women took the game right to China, not letting them out of their half if only for a moment. The Chinese were befuddled, in utter disarray at times. But other moments allowed the Chinese the luxury to connect elegant passes together, showing what they were made of. Indeed, China was a good team, but on this day, the athleticism of the US players took over the game. At times, from a dead start, a US player—I think Press was one—would take a four-stride lead on her opponent. The loose balls won in the midfield were due to constant US pressure and great anticipation, particularly from Lloyd, the eventual goal-scorer, showing off her all-around game.

Absolutely, Lloyd was the leader on the field, setting the tone, winning tackles, setting up the offense, but of particular note was Tobin Heath, number 17. It's as though Arjen Robben and Denilson had a baby sister and raised her from the crib with dribbling skills to unleash onto the Women's World Cup someday. An announcer noted something to the effect of "Heath should give the ball up quicker so that Morgan can display her magic." Morgan, who was coming off an injury, wasn't displaying much magic. Heath was. If anything, Morgan, Lloyd, and all the rest, needed to get the ball to Heath so she could do her thing, which, after she completely dismantled the opposing defense, would bring good results for Morgan, Lloyd, and everyone else. Aside from Lloyd taking care of offense and defense, Heath was flat out the best player on the field. If she had been out of the next match…oh boy. "Just keep her in coach. Better things will happen."

The US had a semi-final date with Germany, the ultra-talented side that defeated France in the other quarterfinal. It was going to be good.

THE 2015 WOMEN'S WORLD CUP
US VS. GERMANY
SEMI-FINALS
2-0

Finally, against China, the US team clicked, playing much better than previous performances in which critics across the board saw something wrong with the chemistry. No one was doing anything or moving forward with positive results; it was hard to watch. And then, against China, in the great rematch of '99, Heath was the player who spun everything together, giving the US side confidence from the dribble, making the opponent look off-balance and at times silly for even trying to be on the same field as her.

The quality of play from Germany and the US was world class from the start. Germany was the world's number one, and the US was rejuvenated and ready to go. Back and forth...there was great possession from both sides, along with technical skill at the highest level. (This match, tallied with the preceding games, marked the most yellow cards in Women's World Cup history, but the play on the field wasn't dirty; at times it was choppy with the referee keeping things under control.)

Rapinoe and Lloyd were strong in the first half, winning tackles while surging forward. The Germans switched fields with remarkable accuracy and pace. The first half reached the highest point with the pass of the game from Heath to Morgan for a one-on-one with Angerer who made a great save. It was one of many saves, as Heath stood out again as the best attacker on the field, creating havoc in the box with multiple attempts at goal.

Moving into the second half, Germany couldn't capitalize on a penalty kick, and controversy struck a few minutes later at the other end when Morgan—who was still a little slow, playing with a previous injury—went down just inside the box, or was it outside? Regardless, she made a great move on the German defender who clearly made the foul leading to a game-winning penalty kick from the captain, Lloyd, who looked left but went right. The subtlety of "looking the wrong way" or even "looking the right way" to throw off a goalie has always been an underappreciated nuance. Whether Lloyd was trying to fool Angerer or not, and whether the keeper was even watching her eyes, is anyone's guess. Some great combination play led to the final goal, putting an extremely talented German side out of the game.

The winner of England and Japan would be irrelevant as this US team was, without a doubt, heading to the first-place podium. With only one goal scored against the US "the whole tournament," it would have taken a miracle to stop this momentum. Eventually Japan won its semi-final. The correct thing for the Japanese to say would have been, "We haven't won the championship yet; we'll take it one game at a time." But please, nothing short of a shootout was going to stop the US. Whether it was England or Japan at that point really didn't matter. The US was on a roll. All Japan could hope for was tying the game.

THE 2015 WOMEN'S WORLD CUP
US VS. JAPAN
CHAMPIONSHIP GAME
5-2

US wins number 3 in great fashion!

The rematch was set to commence. Four short years earlier, in 2011, which may have seemed like an eternity for some of the players, the US lost an agonizing defeat against the talented Japanese in the final match. With all eyes on Vancouver, Canada, the beauty of fate gave everyone another chance to sit back and watch two great teams do it all over again.

As most people know, the game erupted with two early goals from Lloyd, setting the stadium ablaze with excitement. Six minutes hadn't even gone by, and it was 2-0! By the time the third came—still in the first half, mind you—everyone was surprised that it could happen, but it did: Lloyd scored a hat-trick…in the first half. Not only was it a hat-trick, which is rare enough in soccer, it was a hat-trick *in the first half*, and, from a long-distance "chip shot" from half field, as Lloyd capitalized. (This is a shot which many people have tried and failed, only to occur on rare highlight goals from VHS tapes called *101 Great Goals,* and it's done by some Englishman in the mid-80s.) It's worth going over again. Did Lloyd score an amazing long shot to complete a hat-trick in the championship game? Yep. It's the equivalent to an NFL quarterback throwing five or six touchdown passes in the first half of a Super Bowl. *Maybe.* It's hard to compare. The point is, you're not going to see something like this very often. And that made it 4-0. The US was sailing.

Japan, on the other hand, kept things steady, chiseling away at possession, eventually knocking in a goal before the half let out. By the second half, Sawa—Japan's best player from the past—had joined the pitch, hoping to improve the effort. It became 4-2, with Miyama, the talented number eight, leading the way. At this moment, Japan had a chance. With one more goal, the defending champs could have put the US on its heels with an unthinkable comeback. However, Heath found a nice pass at her feet in front of the goal for a guided one-touch score, which took away Japan's momentum.

For soccer fans of "yesteryear," Christie Rampone got subbed in at the young age of 40. Born on June 24, 1975, she completed a cycle of sorts, from the '99 bunch to now. She had played on and off with the national team since 1997 but was left off the memorable '99 roster. From 2003-2009, she took a break from the game, returning all this time later to join Wambach on the stage to hoist the trophy high in the air for a triumphant victory against a worthy rival, bringing a third World Cup title to the United States Women's side.

Sepp Blatter, the president of FIFA at the time, usually presided over the ceremonial functions, but he was absent this time around saying, "...I won't take any travel risks," as he was being investigated by the US Department of Justice for the legal problems he and many of his FIFA colleagues were facing in 2015. This was only a footnote to an otherwise remarkable game as the US team stole the show in fashion, golden confetti and all. To play with such style late in the tournament was a huge turnaround for a team many people were questioning in the early rounds. Analysts noted good play here and there but spoke with trepidation. The talent was there, the potential was there, yet, for a while, the US wasn't "impressing" anybody. Sure, the team had moments of brilliance, but the immediate future was gloomy, at best. Then, from the China match onward, everything clicked as the team was destined to stand in the middle of golden confetti to be compared—rightly so—with the '99 squad, who Lloyd and company had been chasing all this time.

At this point, the team would enjoy the celebrations and get ready for the next Cup in 2019 hosted in amazing France!

APPENDIX

VAR (VIDEO ASSISTANT REFEREE)

Any question as to whether VAR (Video Assistant Referee) should be used in the Women's World Cup is frankly ridiculous. The women's game should have it just as the men's game does. The Women's World Cup is making history, and VAR deserves a place at the table, rightfully so. It's a new technology for soccer. Speaking of the 2018 World Cup in Russia, *CNN* reported, "... this is the first time in history that football has featured VAR at a World Cup."[10]

Very quickly it became a sensation as millions of fans were discussing the pros and cons of advanced refereeing technology. Interestingly, at the 2018 World Cup in Russia, VAR operated like this: From a separate location, a VAR team of four officials viewed the games live with the help of cameras set up around the field. The head referee had a headset which allowed communication with the VAR team. Pretty simple. Information was relayed back and forth. And for important calls, including things like possible goals, ejections, penalty kicks, and offside situations, the technology was encouraged. Furthermore, a head referee has the option of going to a private viewing booth. This is the beauty of VAR.

Goal-line drama is all the rage with VAR. There was the famous situation in the 2010 World Cup down in South Africa that involved Germany and England. It was an elimination game. A huge game. And in the biggest moment of the game, Frank Lampard made what should have been a goal, which would've changed the outcome of the game, and possibly England's whole tournament, and possibly the history of the World Cup, but without VAR, the referees couldn't see in real time what millions of viewers from around the world saw on instant replay: a clear goal. The ball did go over the line. But the physics involved were exacting for even the most experienced referee. Thanks to the ball hitting off the crossbar, then crossing the goal line, then hitting the ground at an angle, the ball then bounced back into the field of play, so it was easy to see how a referee, along with his assistants, could miss such a call in real time. Still, VAR would've been nice to have.

Ejections by way of two yellow cards or a straight red card are huge reasons to have the assistance of the brilliant VAR. Here's one really good example. Let's say a particular player, Jessica, is playing with a yellow card. Then somewhere during a chaotic moment in the game, someone on the opposite team is fouled, and the referee mistakenly thinks that Jessica committed the foul, when, in fact, she didn't. However, the foul is egregious enough for the referee to produce a yellow card, and it turns out to be Jessica's second, which, by the rules of the game, dismisses her, and she has to miss the next match. However, with VAR, the referee can be told by the VAR team that Jessica was innocent after all. And the yellow card will eventually be given to the correct player.

Penalty kicks represent one of the biggest reasons VAR should be used. Was it a foul? Was it not a foul? Ostensibly, VAR can help in this regard. Sometimes a player who is really good at diving might use theatrical liberty to sell a call in the box. At a moment like this, a referee could very well miss the theatrics involved because everything was moving so fast, and in real time it's sometimes hard to distinguish between a real foul and an Oscar-bound player. When everyone at home can see the flop, the referee is in a tough position. Yet, with VAR, the proper call can eventually be made.

If there's a possible offside call, and the referees weren't in position to get it right, then the VAR team can step in and help. Perfect. This assists referees immensely. What needs to be remembered with offside calls is that they represent one of the most difficult calls for referees to make. A player is considered offside if they are behind the last defender at the moment the ball is struck. This is the tricky part. Referees on the field are expected to determine an exact science almost, if we want to call offside such a thing. This is asking a lot of referees. Offside calls can be a really tough thing to get right. Coaches, players, and fans expect referees to get this exactly right every time, and that's an impossible request. Let's recap: The referees have to know exactly when the ball was struck and simultaneously know exactly where the last attacker was at the time of the ball being struck. This is very hard to determine on a regular basis with 100 percent certainty. Add to this, big moments in big games. VAR provides a fantastic option to get important offside calls right.

Some may wonder if VAR is not necessary until the elimination rounds. This is an interesting idea. After all, some of the teams in group play have little chance of success. This is a given. However, the following point is important (and to only say this is *important* is an understatement): Not having VAR in group play might affect teams that may advance far into the tournament. It could successfully be argued that teams like this should have the opportunity to win a group, or place higher in a group, for the sake of placement in the next round.

This makes the discussion of VAR in group play all the more intriguing. Should it be there? Should it wait until the elimination rounds? If we're going to rely on the referees only during group play, then some teams might have room to complain if a call doesn't go the right way. After all, if the fate of a team's tournament is up in the air during a questionable goal-line call in the group stage, then VAR should definitely be present during group games. Waiting to use VAR during the elimination rounds only could deprive a team in the group stage of a chance to move into the elimination rounds. This is why it would make sense to implement VAR from the beginning of the tournament all the way to the end. And again, these points just add to the interesting discussion at large, one which certainly has occupied circles within FIFA.

What's the value of VAR in the first place? Often times, if not all the time, when it comes down to a goal-line call, referees have a hard time knowing if the ball completely went over the line or not. This is the key. Referees cannot be expected to have perfect vision or be in just the right location to make such a critical call every time. Referees are human, which is why the Video Assistant Referee has become so valuable. It's a great tool to use; it only takes a few minutes to double check a call; and by using it, the integrity of the game remains strong. Another strong argument in favor of using VAR is that it takes a lot of pressure off the referees; it's stressful enough officiating a game, and to have the safety net of VAR is good for the overall sanity of referees. They already have fans screaming at them, along with coaches and players. So to have VAR ready, which acts as the ultimate final say on tough decisions, is a good thing for the referees. It allows them room to relax and calmly concentrate on the game in its entirety.

By and large, VAR should be in use. Whether it should be in the group stages or first make an appearance in the eliminations rounds is another question altogether.

PREDICTIONS FOR THE 2019 FIFA WOMEN'S WORLD CUP

Predictions are always a tricky business. Sometimes it's obvious which team will win. Other times, it's a total mystery. Though, when it comes to soccer, predictions can be very interesting. As someone who has made many successful soccer predictions, I can speak to this following point with absolute conviction: Sometimes everything goes completely wrong. It happens. That's the world of predictions. The underdog wins, and the score is way off, and you have no idea how it happened. Or the prediction was exactly right. It should go without saying, but it's worth saying nonetheless: Soccer predictions are unpredictable. Though, sometimes it's not as hard as it looks. And I'd like to think I'm pretty good. When it's right, which I must say is more often than not, the predictions usually have a lot to do with the following criteria: star power, recent team history, overall team history, current injuries, coaches, location, uniforms, the type of training structure each country has, the type of game (i.e., is it a group match or an elimination game?), and, not to mention, a good hunch.

Star power has a lot to do with accurate predictions. Who are the leaders of the team? What do they offer? Are the stars offensive or defensive players? How old are they? Stars play a huge role in the outcomes of games and the overall result of a tournament like the World Cup. So to say they play an important role in determining the outcome of a prediction is a complete understatement. For instance, if Michelle Akers is on a particular team…bet on that team. Then, if somehow Mia Hamm is on that very same team… bet on that team. If you really want to go further, and you realize that not only are Michelle Akers and Mia Hamm on the same team, but there's also Julie Foudy, Kate Sobrero, someone named Kristine Lilly, and Joy Fawcett, then what are you waiting for? Go put money on that team! Every time!

Recent team history is very important for obvious reasons and should not be overlooked. If a team is on a roll, then it usually is a good thing, and you want to take that into consideration for predictions. However, you have to watch closely because sometimes a team might be on a roll after royally defeating less talented teams in friendlies, for example. Be cautious and also realize that good teams going through slumps might be a good thing for that particular team in question. Sometimes good teams need a slump to get jumpstarted back in the right direction. Of course, in this type of scenario, you'd have to consider other factors, which include whether or not the team in a slump has legitimate star players, the age of the players, the style of play the team uses, and so on.

Overall team history is very important. It's also a little mysterious, and, maybe for this reason I like it the best. You see, even though you might be looking at two completely different teams, with completely different players, and a 20-year gap might even be in between the teams in question, they still get similar results. It's like an invisible force that transcends time. (For example: The USWNT of the 1990s and the USWNT of today are both considered a number one team, and the results are similar.) Though, it should be pointed out, that it's not as mysterious as it may originally seem. What happens is, over time the veterans from an older team end up coaching and pass on their ideas of how the game should be played, and, hence, a certain style is established. This is one element as to how teams of different eras can play alike and get similar results. There is also a psychological element involved. An edge that players get from just putting a certain uniform on. Take the United States, for example. Since the US has already won past World Cups, this carries with it a certain confidence and swagger. In other words, when new players are called up to the USWNT, those players know that they're the best of the best. There's no doubt in their minds. They're representing a country that has World Cup titles. There's a history there. So when they put on that US jersey, they are endowed with a certain confidence over other teams. A swagger. Vice versa, when a player from a less talented national team puts on their respected jersey, it should indeed be a special moment, and a proud one at that, but there isn't the same confidence that goes along with it. This is partially why overall team histories matter when making predictions.

Current injuries—and past injuries, for that matter—play a role in how a team performs. This is a pretty commonsense factor worth considering, but it's not always accurate. For instance, during the 2015 World Cup in Canada, Alex Morgan was coming off an injury and wasn't 100 percent. The US still won the whole thing. Injuries matter, but sometimes players can overcome them.

Coaches obviously have a lot to do with how well a team plays. If we're at a tournament, any tournament, and you tell me Anson Dorrance is coaching one of the teams, I'm immediately going to assume that his team will likely win the tournament in question. It's that simple. I know he recruits well. On top of that, I know his approach to the game. He's a brilliant coach, and coaching matters.

The location is important. For instance, in the men's game, prior to World Cup 2014, a European team had not won a World Cup on South American soil. Germany was the first to break through with its championship over Argentina, which was hosted in Brazil. Furthermore, home-field advantage plays a factor. Therefore, host nations often have an edge over opponents. Also, teams that are from a country nearby might perform better because their fans can easily travel to the games. For example, during World Cup 2019 in France, it would make sense that European teams might have a slight advantage over non-European teams, given that their fans have an easy trip to games. (Of course, this advantage has its limits, especially if a team has a very low ranking.)

Uniforms. First of all, fashion matters in sports. Hence, uniforms matter. This is fact. We'll return to this momentarily. Secondly, let me just say this: I'm a fashion guy. I can't help it. I didn't choose to be one. I just am. Basically, my mom took me shopping all the time growing up, and she's originally from LA, a fashion leader in the world, and she definitely knew how to put outfits together, so I know a little something about the field. (Ann Taylor—which was very popular in the 80s—is a store I spent far too much time in; I'll leave it at that.) Back to sports. Uniforms matter in sports. In essence, players will perform based on how they feel, and how they feel has a lot to do with what they're wearing. Are you telling me that if a team wore overalls during a game, they'd perform normally? Okay, case closed. Fashion does matter. In addition to this, there has been scores of scientific research which has shown that what people wear really does affect how they view themselves, think of themselves, and act in general. So yes, fashion does affect human behavior, and I contend it affects how players perform in sports.

I'll use an example from the Men's World Cup in 2018. Germany had its traditional look of white-black-white (a white shirt, black shorts, white socks). From the outset this is fine. Don't get me wrong, a basic, simple uniform is often the best thing to trigger the best possible performance out of players. Traditionally, Germany has had a nice, simple uniform. However, adidas was the sponsor for Germany in 2018, and the particular design that adidas provided for many, if not all, of its teams had three stripes on the shoulders of the uniforms. In Germany's case, it was three black stripes on the shoulders of a white uniform which really stood out, in a non-flowing way. The fashion sense of this choice was just off, there's no other way to put it. It's hard to explain but it just wasn't working. (From the beginning I had a feeling that it was going to negatively affect the way the players played. It was a feeling of trepidation, if you will. And we're talking about one simple design flaw, something that would drive Tim Gunn crazy.) From the get-go, Germany wasn't playing right. And, low and behold, things didn't go well for the Germans. In fact, Germany, the defending champs, couldn't even get out of its group. And on top of that, its play was less than inspiring, just like its uniforms.

Now, did Germany's bad result have everything to do with the uniforms? No, absolutely not. But I strongly believe that the uniforms had something to do with the result. How much is debatable. So in essence, uniforms matter, and if something is out of sync with a particular design, it might affect how a team plays.

The type of training structure each country has is very important. By "training structure," I am referring to a country's overall soccer infrastructure. So you have to ask yourself: What sort of training structure does each country have? And by country I literally mean all levels of soccer pertaining to a country, and not just a particular national team. I'm focusing on a country's overall training structure because this determines how youth players are trained growing up, which also determines, eventually, how they'll play at the national team level. So, therefore, a country's overall soccer infrastructure (i.e., its training structure) is a vital component, and it's a strong indicator of how a particular national team will perform.

The type of game being played is also important. In other words, is it a group match or an elimination game? Sometimes star players sit out and rest during group matches. So if it's a group match, you never know. Elimination games are more important, so in most cases, star players will be on the field. Also, some teams have a track record of not fairing well in elimination games. Things like this have to be taken into consideration.

Lastly, let's not forget a good old hunch. In other words, common sense. Sometimes you just have a feeling about a game, and you go with it.

With all these factors combined, you have the reasoning behind the predictions. All in all, predictions should be a lot of fun while they also provide useful information for fans about the players and teams.

Now let's get into the predictions, shall we?

Group A
France (1)
Norway (2)
South Korea (3)
Nigeria (4)

France will likely win Group A, with Norway coming in a close second. I suspect France will have three wins and zero losses, or, quite possibly two wins and a tie (the tie coming from Norway). France's star, Amandine Henry, should have something to do with a few of the goals, even if she's not directly involved as the scorer or assist-maker; she'll likely play a role in some form as the attack is created with an "assist to an assist" type of thing.

Led by its star player, Maren Mjelde, Norway should essentially defeat both South Korea and Nigeria, while taking a tie or loss from its game with France. Thus, Norway will finish in second.

South Korea will probably suffer two losses, from France and Norway, and gain a tie from Nigeria. Hence, South Korea should finish in third place. Although Ji Soyun might help the cause, it looks unlikely that South Korea will escape its group.

Nigeria will probably have a tie with South Korea and two losses from France and Norway. Asisat Oshoala could very well have some good games, but Nigeria is likely exiting the tournament after its last group game is complete.

Group B
Germany (1)
China (2)
Spain (3)
South Africa (4)

Germany, led by its star Dzsenifer Marozsan, will not be defeated in group play. The only scenario in which Germany suffers a defeat, or even a tie, will be against the supremely talented Chinese. Outside of this possibility, Germany is too talented, and the team has something to prove this tournament, even more than before. Furthermore, the tantalizing reality of a third World Cup title is within grasp, and Germany will do everything it can to make this dream come true. Therefore, Germany gains three wins in Group B, thus winning the group.

China will suffer a loss from Germany and gain two wins over Spain and South Africa. Li Ying should have solid opening games.

Spain will take two defeats from Germany and China, while enjoying a victory over South Africa. Spain's coach Jorge Vilda and its star player Irene Paredes will not get the results they were hoping for.

South Africa, despite its best effort, will take three losses and finish last in the group. South Africa's star player Janine van Wyk and its coach Desiree Ellis will put forward a good effort but will walk away empty handed.

Group C
Australia (1)
Brazil (2)
Italy (3)
Jamaica (4)

The favorite to win Group C is very unclear. This group is gearing up to be tricky, to say the least. Let's go with Australia as the winner. With the help of its star player, Sam Kerr, it should defeat Jamaica and Italy and tie Brazil.

Brazil, though, could also win the group, but I'm going to place them in second. Brazil should tie Australia. Then, I suspect, Brazil will defeat Italy and Jamaica. Watch out, though. It could play down to the competition and struggle with Jamaica…but Brazil should walk away with a victory. Marta will show well initially, though she might not be as impactful as she was in previous years.

Italy, led by its star player, Barbara Bonansea, will come in third with losses to Brazil and Australia, along with a victory over Jamaica. However, with that said, Italy is the trickiest element in this group. I could very well see the Italians winning the whole group outright, but something tells me otherwise. Keep an eye on Italy. If I'm wrong about this prediction, I'll be the first to admit it.

Good old Jamaica, an island nation with a lot of heart and character, will most likely, almost certainly, lose all three games. This is Jamaica's first Women's World Cup appearance, and, you never know, it might be its last. Its star player, Jody Brown, might have a good showing, but, all in all, she and her coach, Hue Menzies, will be exiting the tournament after only three games.

Group D
Japan (1)
England (2)
Scotland (3)
Argentina (4)

Outside of a major turnaround from the past two successful World Cups, I'm willing to bet Japan will win Group D with two wins and a tie. It should likely defeat Scotland and Argentina. The tie should come against England. Mana Iwabuchi should have a good opening three games; expect more from her in the elimination rounds.

England, led by its star Fran Kirby, should come in second with two ties and a win. The ties should come against Japan and Scotland. England should easily wipe the floor with Argentina, attaining a big win.

Scotland and its star player Kim Little will likely come in third with a win over Argentina, a loss to Japan, and a draw with England.

Argentina will be out in three games with three losses. Despite a good effort from its star player, Estefania Banini, Argentina will be back on a plane thinking about what went wrong and how to fix things for the future.

Group E
Canada (1)
Netherlands (2)
Cameroon (3)
New Zealand (4)

Canada and its star player Christine Sinclair should get first place in this group, with two easy wins against Cameroon and New Zealand, along with a tie against the Netherlands. Canada's coach, Kenneth Heiner-Moller, will have a lot to work with after viewing his team in the group stage and gearing up for the elimination rounds. Christine Sinclair should play average to well with a hint of things to come.

The Netherlands will likely get a draw with Canada, along with two wins over Cameroon and New Zealand. Watch for Lieke Martens to be instrumental in these opening tests. Her play, and that of her team, will likely please coach Sarina Wiegman heading into the elimination rounds.

Cameroon will most likely earn third place after suffering two defeats against Canada and the Netherlands. Yet Cameroon should salvage a close win over New Zealand. Cameroon's star player Gabrielle Onguene might have a good showing, but three games will be it for the West African women.

New Zealand will end up in fourth place after three defeats. Ali Riley, the team's star player, will likely have a few good moments, but that'll be all she wrote for New Zealand. Coach Tom Sermanni will have to rethink things on the long plane ride home to New Zealand.

Group F
United States (1)
Sweden (2)
Chile (3)
Thailand (4)

The United States has a pretty easy group. That is, it's a pretty easy group outside of Sweden, which will be the biggest challenge. In fact, don't be surprised to see the US take a loss from the Swedes. However, the USWNT should win all three games and finish number one in the group. Tobin Heath and Alex Morgan should have big games while coach Jill Ellis will have her work cut out for her going into the elimination rounds where things won't be as easy. (By the way, expect triumphant, heavy-handed scores against Chile and Thailand; don't be surprised to see Morgan get a hat-trick against both teams.)

Coach Peter Gerhardsson will lead Sweden to a second-place finish after suffering a loss to the US. The Swedes should easily defeat both Chile and Thailand. Stina Blackstenius, one of the team's star players, will probably have at least three goals in total by the end of the third game.

In third place will be Chile, with two losses (taken from the US and Sweden) and a close win over Thailand. Christiane Endler, the team's goalie, will have good moments in front of the net, but it won't be enough to finish in the top two places.

Despite a good effort from its star player Kanjana Sungngoen, along with well-thought-out strategy from its coach Nuengruethai Sathongwien, Thailand will finish in last place with three losses.

Round of 16

(From here on out, the teams are not organized officially as it is too soon to determine who plays who. The predictions are simply for who will win and move on.)

France (win)
Norway (win)
Germany (win)
China (win)

Canada (win)
Netherlands (loss)
United States (win)
Sweden (win)

Australia (loss)
Brazil (win)
Japan (win)
England (loss)

South Korea (loss)
Spain (loss)
Italy (loss)
Scotland (loss)

Quarterfinals
France (win)
Norway (win)
Germany (win)
China (win)
Brazil (loss)
Japan (win)
Canada (loss)
United States (win)
Sweden (loss)

Semi-finals
Germany (win)
China (loss)
Japan (loss)
United States (win)

Consolation match
Fourth: China
Third: Japan

Final
Second: Germany
First: United States

PROSPECTIVE WORLD CUP LOCATIONS

Hosting a World Cup is a great honor. Without a doubt, the act of doing so is coveted around the world. So many nations would like to be considered by FIFA for such an opportunity. The economy gets a boost...usually anyway. The tourism for the event is great. The prestige it renders to a nation is great. Hosting a World Cup is an act that goes down in the history books. It's like the World's Fair or the Olympics.

When a nation hosts a World Cup, people around the world automatically associate that country with the year of the World Cup. China 1991, Sweden 1995, the United States 1999, the United States 2003, China 2007, Germany 2011, Canada 2015, and France 2019. Each country holds a special place at the elite table of nations that have hosted. Hosting a World Cup should also, theoretically, add a boost to the prestige of a nation's soccer program, which, in turn, should filter down to the youth, collegiate, and professional levels. Local economies get extra business; games are played on TV, giving host cities exposure, which theoretically should be good for business down the road. It's a win-win for everyone.

Let's take a look at potential countries that might host a World Cup down the road. There are so many to choose from, with so many ups and downs, pros and cons. Where to start?

China. It has hosted twice before. This could potentially be a drawback. Hosting too many times takes away some of the allure of the festivities. Been there, done that, is a common sentiment. It might be good to stay away from places that have hosted on more than one occasion; this is to say, stay away from these places in the immediate future; far down the line, after many other new countries have hosted, places like China and the United States should be considered again. On the flip side, China is a likable host nation. Traditionally, China has a rich history that dates back thousands of years, bringing with it prestige. Currently, it's a leader on the world scene. It has mega-cities, with interesting places to visit, and great food with historical value. Transportation is widely available in the cities. Furthermore, of valuable importance, the China women's national team is a major player in the international soccer scene. This definitely adds value as China represents Asia at large as one of the leading soccer-playing nations for women. (Japan also shares this honor.)

Laos, by comparison, would not be a good nation to host a World Cup. For starters, women's soccer in Laos is virtually nonexistent. The city structure within Laos is not nearly as developed as China's. Tourism in Laos is less than desirable. So, therefore, fans visiting a hypothetical World Cup would not have superior hotel accommodations afforded to them, nor would they have the advantageous ability to travel around like they would in China or the United States. Stadiums. It's a country that also lacks the proper stadiums for such an event.

Much of the same could be said of Cambodia, especially when it comes to its women's soccer program. Laos and Cambodia, two virtually nonexistent players in the international soccer scene, need to improve their overall soccer programs before ever being considered as a potential host nation for a World Cup. Furthermore, Cambodia does not have the necessary infrastructure needed to host such a grand event; the hotels, travel accommodations, and stadiums do not fit the correct criteria. However, Cambodia has many things going for it, which draw tourists from around the world: the food, interesting culture, and, arguably the most alluring element about Cambodia, the historic architecture of Angkor Wat and related sites. While the rich, historic, mysterious, astronomical, enchanting, and educational features of Angkor Wat represent Cambodia in the best light possible, it just doesn't account for the country's drawbacks when it comes to considering it as a host for the World Cup in the modern era. And with this in mind, Cambodia is out. Next.

Thailand would seem like a perfect and enchanting location to host a World Cup. And, for all intents and purposes, it might someday be such a place for the FIFA Women's World Cup. Arguably, Thailand is the premiere tourist destination of Southeast Asia. There are many locations—including Bangkok, Chang Mai, Hat Yai, Pattaya, Nakhon Ratchasima, Udon Thani, and Khon Kaen—but most the cities are not very large in scope, giving the event somewhat of a downgraded feel to it. On top of that, stadiums would be an issue in Thailand; there need to be stadiums with state-of-the-art seating capacity for a huge endeavor such as the World Cup; while Thailand may fit this criteria in some cases, it may need to upgrade here and there, which is not out of the realm of possibility. In terms of hotels, traveling, and food, Thailand is a good—but not great—location to consider. In terms of culture and history and sightseeing, Thailand is a phenomenal location, one that should be given serious consideration down the line. One drawback would be its soccer program in general. The women's national team of Thailand has limited World Cup experience. To say it's a program on the rise would be putting it politely. In terms of women's soccer, Thailand has a lot of room for growth and improvement. The team has been pushing for more funding, and with recent success in Asia, things should be improving on that level. But overall, soccer isn't the biggest headline when people think of Thailand. They think of great food, remarkable history, astounding culture, and a beautiful place for vacation, not women's soccer. This needs to improve. With that said, Thailand has so much to offer, and it would be a very interesting place to host the Women's World Cup in the near future.

Experience plays a role as well. Have Laos, Cambodia, or Thailand hosted a big event such as the Olympics or a World Cup before? No. And that is a problem.

Japan is a likely destination for the FIFA Women's World Cup. In fact, Japan is a shoe-in; it's a perfect host. It has already hosted—well, co-hosted with South Korea—the 2002 FIFA World Cup for the men. It is a leading nation in the world with a thriving economy, an advanced city structure, quality airports, highly advanced transportation, up-to-scale hotel accommodations, spectacular cuisine, and a rich history to boot. It's clean and safe, which all adds to a perfect vacation destination. Furthermore, Japan has up-to-date facilities for training, and its stadiums are equipped with the proper infrastructure and capacity to sustain a World Cup. On top of that, Japan's soccer program for both men and women is elevated above the rest of Asia. It doesn't hurt that the women's team of Japan won the 2011 World Cup and placed second in 2015. In fact, this would put Japan over the top as the leading Asian nation for women's soccer, which it is (alongside China). This is crucial: When people think of Japan, soccer comes to mind. This is one of the key elements to hosting a World Cup. All in all, Japan is a perfect location for hosting a FIFA World Cup and expect to see it doing so in the near future.

South Korea is a potential host. However, it's a small country—both in terms of geography and the stadiums it has to offer—and it would likely have to co-host with Japan for optimal success, just as it did for the 2002 FIFA World Cup. Seoul, Daegu, Incheon, Gwangju, and Busan are good locations, but, again, the idea of co-hosting with Japan is probably best.

India is an interesting candidate. First off, let's recognize that India is probably not going to be awarded a FIFA Women's World Cup, but it's worth considering. Why won't it? Well, soccer in India just isn't a big deal, and, in particular, women's soccer in India is not very well known. In terms of hosting a Women's World Cup, it would be similar to South Africa hosting the Men's World Cup in 2010. South Africa is not a leading soccer nation in the men's game. It's just not. Though it did provide an interesting place for the tournament. And, it put Africa on the map for finally hosting a World Cup. Likewise, India would be an interesting place for such an event, and it would help put soccer on the map both for India and Asia at large. India is a large country with big cities, but hotels and transportation could be an issue moving forward. Additionally, the issue of providing adequate stadiums might be a contentious conversation. And, frankly, to reiterate, soccer just isn't that big a draw in India (i.e., it's not known for soccer). To reflect the world's game in a positive image, it might not be the best location to host. Right now, the numbers just don't add up. Not even if Ramanujan was doing the calculation.

Malaysia. It's not a place that immediately comes to mind for hosting a Women's World Cup. But then again, why not? Could Malaysia possibly co-host with Thailand? They are neighbors. It might make sense. Malaysia is a vacation destination. A few cities worth mentioning include that of Johor Bahru, Ipoh, and Kuala Lumpur. Perhaps it's not quite the destination Thailand is, but it's a destination nonetheless. Without a doubt, proper and modern stadiums in Malaysia, or lack thereof, are definitely going to be a drawback. Another big drawback would be its women's soccer program…or lack thereof. On its own, Malaysia might constitute an interesting, exotic, and memorable place for such a tournament, but in the grand scheme of things, it would need a partner like Thailand to assist in such an endeavor. Here's a possibility: a triumvirate of Thailand-Singapore-Malaysia. Possible, though not likely.

Australia would be high on the list. There's a lot of potential with the big country Down Under. It has the experience of hosting the Olympics, which is a major plus. It's a developed nation with quality airports, ground transportation, hotels, restaurants, and stadiums. The women's team of Australia is growing in quality and is definitely a program on the rise. Things are swinging heavily in Australia's favor. A possibility might include a joint hosting effort between Australia and its neighbor, New Zealand. That's worth consideration, but Australia hosting alone would probably be more ideal.

Angola, Namibia, Botswana, Zambia, Zimbabwe, Mozambique… all interesting places with enormous potential down the road. I don't know when that would be exactly, but let's focus on South Africa, shall we? First off, South Africa hosted a successful 2010 World Cup for the men's side. It represented the first, history-making, World Cup that took place in Africa. This was something FIFA really wanted to accomplish, and by including Africa in 2010 and Asia in 2002, FIFA was expanding the overall reach of soccer throughout the world, which was a great idea. And FIFA delivered on this. South Africa was an exotic, interesting, and exciting location for the 2010 World Cup. Bringing the FIFA

Women's World Cup to its borders is absolutely within the realm of possibility.

However, one drawback from the 2010 World Cup was the expensive all-around cost for travelers departing from the Americas, Asia, and Europe. Another drawback, quite honestly, included the vuvuzelas, which proved so annoying that some people tried to have them banned from the games, an effort which eventually proved unsuccessful. Nonetheless, many people felt that the loud horns obstructed a certain part of the games which otherwise would have been more enjoyable. If South Africa were to host a Women's World Cup, would the vuvuzelas be a distraction yet again? Should FIFA take such a thing under consideration before making a decision? All in all, apart from the vuvuzelas echoing throughout the stadiums, the 2010 World Cup proved to be a good one, and South Africa represents an interesting place for a future Women's World Cup, thus making it a strong candidate down the road.

East Africa has a few candidates, the primary one being Ethiopia. However, when it comes to women's soccer, Ethiopia is just not on par with the rest of the world. Though Ethiopia might represent an interesting location down the line, it currently lacks an in-depth soccer presence for such an event. The same can be said of Kenya, another possible East African candidate. An interesting possibility rests in a co-hosting partnership between Ethiopia and Kenya. Such an event would be great for the development of women's soccer, and soccer in general, for the area. That aside, generally speaking, East Africa has a lot going for it: The countryside is beautiful, the food is unique and wonderful, and the people are accommodating. Without a doubt, it's a region with an amazing amount of potential that should be considered down the road.

West Africa is a vibrant place that has a few women's soccer teams that are flourishing, which include Nigeria and Cameroon at the top of the list. West Africa is a region that loves soccer, and the passion it exudes certainly will make it a prime candidate down the road. One issue would be proper stadiums for a huge event like the Women's World Cup. As such a thing improves, or if FIFA can work out deals to construct modern stadiums on par with France, the most recent host, then who knows. We might possibly have a World Cup in Cameroon, or possibly Morocco. However, Morocco is a place that is considered to be more a part of North Africa than West, despite its geographic positioning which seems to put it in both. Regardless, this brings us to North Africa.

The expansive, majestic, land of North Africa. Morocco, Algeria, Tunisia, Libya, and Egypt would be the main contenders for hosting a Women's World Cup in North Africa. Here's a quick drawback for these possible candidates: None of them are very well known when it comes to women's soccer. Having said that, of these possible candidates, the best equipped would likely be Egypt. Though Morocco would be divine. Many people can't say enough goods things about the mysterious land overlooking the Atlantic that has a legendary movie—*Casablanca*—connected to it. However, Egypt might just surpass such competition on the immediate list of places in North Africa to host a successful and eventful World Cup.

After all, Egypt is, with a doubt, one of the most amazing places on earth, if not the most amazing. (Though such debates are neither here nor there.) The amount of history that ancient Egypt has to offer is practically limitless, and new things—particularly in the world of archaeology—are being found even to this day.

The Great Pyramids of Giza, the Sphinx, Luxor, and so many other aspects of Egypt render it a unique, mysterious, exotic, educational, entertaining, and breathtaking location. Adding a Women's World Cup to just a tiny portion of Egypt's culture and vast history would be a win-win for everyone. If the ancient library of Alexandria were still standing in its original form, a collection of a Women's World Cup hosted by Egypt—the land of Sobekneferu, Hatshepsut, Nefertiti, and Cleopatra—would absolutely be a rich addition to its immaculate collection. Yes to Egypt; hopefully it'll get a Women's World Cup someday soon. Let's recap: breathtaking Egypt, mysterious Morocco, vibrant Cameroon, possibly an intriguing Ethiopia–Kenya partnership, and beautiful South Africa are ideal options for a future Women's World Cup.

Iran, Iraq, Saudi Arabia, and other Middle Eastern countries represent interesting places with potential to host a Women's World Cup down the road.

South America is a wide-open frontier yet to be explored for hosting a FIFA Women's World Cup. Argentina might be one of the little gems out there yet to host the tournament. It has all the intangibles: a pretty landscape, a soccer-rich history, stadiums, magnificent food, a controversial ambassador of the game who is nonetheless great for the game (referring, of course, to Maradona), and the experience of hosting a previous World Cup, albeit the men's competition back in 1978.

Is Argentina due to host another World Cup, one for the women? The answer is undoubtedly and resoundingly yes. One simple drawback: The Argentinian women's national team is far from great, and, in fact, it's a team struggling to find its way, with some success here and there. It's not all bad for Argentina, but it's nowhere near the caliber of Germany or the United States, that's for sure. In short, Argentina would be a great host nation for the women's game, and this may be a reality sooner than we think.

Uruguay, the great Uruguay, is another possible location worth speculation. Indeed, without a doubt, Uruguay is a bit small to host. But is this a problem? Geographically? Should it be an issue? If anything, a small nation like Uruguay is accessible and easy to travel within; unlike Canada, whereby the games were often vast distances apart, Uruguay would be, for lack of a better word, somewhat comfortable. Montevideo, Salto, Ciudad de la Costa, and Paysandu are ready to go. Uruguay's stadiums are presumably suitable for the stature of a Women's World Cup, and, if some of the stadiums are not up to specification, then certainly construction can be done to get things to a satisfactory level. In terms of potentially hosting the Women's World Cup, Uruguay, from the outset, receives a C+, maybe a B-. Whereas, Argentina, its direct neighbor, receives a B+ on average.

As for Paraguay, Bolivia, and Peru: These places might need a little time before stepping into the discussion of hosting a World Cup. Their close South American neighbor Chile, however, is another prime candidate for hosting. Chile, of all places, should be higher on the list.

First, Chile has the experience of hosting the Men's World Cup of 1962. By and large, that was regarded as a great tournament that took off without a hitch. Theoretically, the same result could occur for the women's game, and in today's age, Chile seems like an ideal location with its wineries, food, accommodating people, beautiful landscape, and a passion for soccer. However, like Argentina, the women's national team of Chile is growing in quality, but it's a team that is looking to assert itself in a bigger way internationally. So therefore, Chile has a lot going for it in terms of checking off the boxes for a yes down the road to hosting a Women's World Cup.

Brazil has a thriving women's national team, a rich tradition in world soccer and the experience of hosting multiple big-time sporting events, including the 1958 and 2014 Men's World Cups, and the 2016 Olympics (held in Rio). The 2014 World Cup was regarded by many people as one of the best in recent history. There's no reason to think the same couldn't happen for the Women's World Cup. Brazil has the infrastructure to support such an event, and the passion is there for the women's side of things, which gives it a thumbs-up. There's no reason, really, why Brazil shouldn't host. It likely will, and don't be surprised to see that happen sometime soon.

Colombia and Venezuela. Tough call. As Carson Kressley would say co-hosting the Miss Universe 2018 pageant, (paraphrasing), "It's not a Miss Universe pageant without Miss Venezuela." The same is not really said for women's soccer. This would probably apply to Colombia as well. Pretty much across the board, both nations are not big on women's soccer and for the most part this would exclude them from hosting such a tournament.

Central American nations including Panama, Costa Rica, Nicaragua, Honduras, Guatemala, Belize, and El Salvador probably need a little time to prepare stadiums and the infrastructure to support a Women's World Cup; not to mention, women's soccer in these countries is not up to par with competitive nations. However, to promote women's soccer in Central America, which would be a positive move in the right direction, hosting a World Cup would be a great start. Costa Rica is a likely candidate. It's a vacation destination, with hotels, nightlife, and great restaurants. Another idea to put forward is that of a co-hosting possibility. Perhaps Guatemala, Honduras, and Costa Rica could share the responsibility. It would be a step in the right direction for women's soccer in Central America, that's for sure. It's a beautiful area, with amazing culture, history, and food. These nations have potential possibly down the road but as for now it will have to wait.

Mexico. Why not Mexico? Mexico is beautiful, exotic, and centrally located. It has hosted two men's World Cups in 1970 and 1986. It would be logical to host the Women's World Cup as well. It's definitely a place with great potential. However, there are a few drawbacks. With the exception of a place like Japan, where crime is almost non-existent, most countries are going to have crime in one way or another. Mexico has been exceeding a normal limit for acceptable crime levels in recent years. There have been stories, including this 2018 report from *The Economist*, that indicate approximately 30,000 crime-related deaths will likely occur in a given year. "Some 25,340 Mexicans, says the government, were murdered last year, well above the previous peak of 2011. The toll for 2018 is on track to pass 30,000. Why is Mexico's murder rate rocketing?

Mexico has the misfortune to lie directly between South America's coca fields and the United States, the world's biggest drug market. The drugs trade created criminal gangs who fight over turf and kill those who try to stop them doing business. Guns, easily bought in the United States, flow back into Mexico. Weak law enforcement lets gangsters kill with virtual impunity."[11]

Crime of this sort is not only found in Mexico; it's a worldwide problem that authorities deal with on a daily basis. And this isn't to say that such issues would directly affect a Women's World Cup, but at the same time an institution like FIFA surely takes such a thing into serious consideration. Gang related or not, 30,000 is an alarming amount. Isn't 10,000 a lot? We're talking about 30,000. Sure, this is largely within the element of a gang world, and a beautiful event like the World Cup is supposed to alleviate such concerns from peoples' minds, but, nonetheless, this is a factor to take under consideration, one that members of FIFA are certainly aware of.

With that said, there's so much that Mexico has to offer when it comes to beautiful scenery, exotic hotels, amazing authentic food, rich culture, history, along with unique archaeological sites which showcase the ancient cultures of the Aztecs, Zapotecs, and Toltecs. Add to this, soccer is Mexico's biggest sport. It's a culture. It's a way of life in Mexico. Though women's soccer is on the rise, the all-around love and passion for the sport makes it a great, and almost perfect, location for the biggest women's tournament on earth.

Bermuda, the Bahamas, and the Virgin Islands might not represent the highest quality women's soccer around the block, but they would be an interesting partnership in co-hosting the Women's World Cup. Each place represents a beautiful island vacation dream come true, and, given that proper stadiums are lined up, such an idea might be worth considering in the future. Jamaica alone might be a location worth thinking over. Like its Caribbean neighbors, it's got the elements of a perfect vacation which would entice tourists to take in a World Cup. It might not be at the top of the list, but Jamaica would certainly be a memorable place worth considering.

The United States is an obvious choice for another World Cup. The problem, though, is that it has already hosted two times. In fact, the US hosted in 1999 and then directly again in 2003! A bit much, don't you think? For this reason, the hosting responsibilities need to be spread out a bit more. Give it some time, and the US should be back in the saddle and hosting again down the road.

Why is the United States such a good host? First, the USWNT is the best in the world. This has created a huge following. The passion, excitement, and fan enthusiasm is undeniable. Women's soccer is huge in America, and this transcends to ticket sales, plain and simple. If the US hypothetically hosted the 2019 World Cup, there would have been a frenzy for USWNT tickets and those would have sold out very quickly.

Second, the infrastructure of the United States is a standard around the world. People move to the US for good reason: the economy is usually good, transportation is great on most all levels, hotels are abundant, and restaurants aren't that bad either. Additionally, the stadiums are top class and offer a wide spectrum of capacities, which is very important. For smaller games between two teams that don't have that big of a draw, maybe receiving only 20,000 fans, there are stadiums available which can be predetermined to adjust for the small numbers. For larger games, such as a championship, there are huge stadiums that, again, can be predetermined. There are also plenty of great nightlife activities in major US cities in which tourists can partake while they're enjoying the World Cup.

Pro soccer in America is alive and well for the women. This clearly and unequivocally adds value. Cities with a pro team are sure to be hotspots for World Cup hysteria, which equals ticket sales. The local economies will thrive. This is good for TV ratings, and this is something each host city has a vested interest in.

The list of cities in the US that would want to feature the Women's World Cup is too long; a few would include New York, Philadelphia, Washington D.C., Charlotte, Miami, Orlando, Atlanta, Cincinnati, Columbus, Nashville, St. Louis, Kansas City, Chicago, Minneapolis, Houston, Dallas, Phoenix, Los Angeles, San Francisco, Portland, and Seattle. Each location offers an ideal soccer-friendly environment that also provides travel accommodations of all kinds. To reiterate, the United States would be on the immediate list of candidates if not for already hosting in 1999 and 2003. With that said, the 20-year anniversary for 2003 is coming up shortly, which is a large enough window of time for the US to jump back into consideration. That is, if others don't make a strong enough argument to host the tournament elsewhere.

Canada obviously just hosted the Women's World Cup in 2015. It produced a great result, a World Cup to go down in history. Should Canada host again, which it probably will, it will have to be a few World Cups down the road to allow others an opportunity. What about the US hosting in 1999 and 2003? Why can't Canada do the same? That was—and should be—a one-time occurrence. Such a thing precludes others from hosting the event, and that's not good for the growth of soccer around the world, nor is it good for the image of the sport. When the US hosted twice in a row, there was a feeling of *here we go again*. It didn't feel as special. Imagine the US hosting three times in a row...there would be a feeling of *there's that tournament again,* and it might as well be called "the United States Tournament of Nations." Part of the charm of the World Cup experience is to showcase a different host nation each time around, which promotes different cultures, which is what the World Cup is all about. That's how it should be. While Canada should be in line to host again in a few cycles, there should be a different nation hosting each time around which is best for everyone involved.

Europe is quite simply the leader of soccer in the world. It does, though, have competition from South America (obviously), North America, Africa (to some extent), the Middle East (to some extent), and Asia. But, without a doubt, Europe represents the cradle of soccer in the world. It's where the sport was invented, and, today, in terms of female club soccer, it's where a vast amount of opportunities is afforded to the best female players (outside of their national team experience). Ireland represents an interesting place for a World Cup. It's an enchanting island, it's a great vacation destination, stadiums are available, and soccer is a passion. Scotland, ditto.

England would be the best candidate from this region. Obviously, soccer was invented in England. The women's game is growing with quality in England by leaps and bounds. It has the infrastructure, the stadiums, and a rich environment perfect for hosting. England has also hosted a number of huge events before, including the 2012 Olympics in London, and the 1966 World Cup. It has been in line to host the Men's World Cup again, and it would make sense for England to host the Women's World Cup as well. What better place is there? Germany.

Quite frankly, each World Cup that Germany has hosted has been as good as it can get. Germany thrives on technological advancement, and its stadiums reflect this. They are state of the art, exuding high quality. The Women's World Cup of

2011 and the Men's World Cup of 2006 were brilliant, and should information about World Cup history be stored in a time capsule, they should be placed at the very top. Germany sits in the heart of Europe, with amazing, historical places to visit, along with authentic cuisine, some of the finest beer in the world, and accommodating and exuberant citizens who live for soccer. Germany, like the United States, has set a standard for how a World Cup should be hosted. The hotels, travel, security, showmanship, and accessibility to media are second to none. Look for Germany to host again after a few cycles.

Norway would be a great location. Its women's team is among the best in the world. This adds much value to potentially hosting. There is a drawback, though. As a place to visit, it's a little expensive for a broad spectrum of tourists, and this may preclude it from eventually taking the honor of hosting, but it has a great backdrop for a World Cup, including the cities of Oslo, Trondheim, and Stavanger, with stadiums and beautiful accommodations. Who knows, possibly down the line a Women's World Cup will land in Norway.

Sweden, of course, hosted in 1995. It's an ideal place to feature a World Cup. There's one reason it shouldn't reclaim the honor: It benefits the game at large if new places are afforded the opportunity to host.

Finland would be an interesting candidate, but, unlike its Scandinavian neighbors, it doesn't excel at soccer, particularly women's soccer, which would hold it back somewhat. Do not take Iceland off the map of consideration. Soccer is gaining momentum on the small island, and it might be worth a second look down the road.

The Netherlands, like Uruguay, is small geographically, but it provides many good reasons to host which include stadiums, easy travel, a fun atmosphere with cities like Amsterdam, Rotterdam, and Utrecht, along with a soccer-rich environment whereby the women's team is doing well internationally.

Belgium might not have the best women's team in the world, but it's similar to the Netherlands in its size and capability to host a Women's World Cup. The cities of Antwerp, Ghent, and Brussels are an asset. It would be a fascinating place for the tournament, and it might be one to watch for down the road. Liechtenstein and Luxemburg are just too small; the geography does not work in their favor.

Poland, Estonia, Latvia, Lithuania, Belarus, Ukraine, Moldova, Romania, Slovakia, Czech Republic, Hungary, Slovenia, Croatia, Bosnia and Herzegovina, Montenegro, Kosovo, Albania, Macedonia, and Bulgaria might be interesting locations, and down the line they should be considered. For now, though, a small neighbor might be worth stronger consideration: Switzerland. Switzerland hosted the 1954 Men's World Cup; a long time ago, yes, but experience nonetheless. Like Uruguay, the Netherlands, and Belgium, it's a little confined. Its biggest drawback would probably be that its women's soccer program is not well known. Austria's biggest drawback is that of Switzerland: Women's soccer in Austria is less known, and a place with a better female soccer program would be more ideal.

Portugal is hit or miss. It has a great setting with the cities of Lisbon, Porto, and Braga serving as good assets. Its women's soccer program isn't much to speak of; however, it has been known for hosting the Algarve Cup, which is an international soccer tournament for women, adding value to its experience with the women's game. Portugal! Why not? It seems like a good fit!

Italy has a women's team that is gaining stature throughout international soccer. The Italians hosted the 1934 and 1990 World Cups for the men, which is an added bonus. Italy lives and breathes soccer, another added bonus. It's a beautiful country, rich with history, an ideal tourist destination, and it clearly has the stadiums to host a Women's World Cup.

Greece is not well-regarded for women's soccer on the international scene, but it has plenty of virtues to keep it on the table. Like Egypt, Greece has a rich ancient history. It offers endless possibilities for tourists. It hosted the original Olympics, therefore making it an icon in the arena of hosting a sporting event. It's such a classic place, and the cities of Athens, Thessaloniki, Patras, and Volos only give it more value and charm.

Russia and Turkey. These are possible candidates. Russia pulled off a successful presentation of the 2018 World Cup and surely could accomplish the same for the women. However, there were doubts that Russia could do such a good job in 2018. Some people thought there might be political unrest, or some kind of violence in the streets from protesters and the like. Yet, no such thing occurred. Turkey, on the other hand, has not hosted a World Cup for the men or women. Russia and Turkey may have to wait in line a little bit, but they're definitely possible candidates. It's a long line.

It's a prestigious honor to host the FIFA Women's World Cup. One that many nations hope to receive.

CLOSING WORDS

Well, here we go again: another beautiful tournament. The illustrious Women's World Cup. It keeps getting better each time. There is arguably the same excitement for the women's tournament as there is for the men's. If not, it's getting there. The Women's World Cup has a special vibe about it. Over the years, it has gained in popularity. It's become a worldwide sensation, one that draws millions of people to TV sets to catch a glimpse of history in the making from some of the most talented female athletes in the world.

Thus far, the 1999 World Cup has built up an allure that has been difficult for any future World Cup to duplicate. Though, it can be successfully argued, that 1999 has provided inspiration for each and every team. It also created a standard, and, not to mention, a perfect memory in history, a reminder of how great the sport is. The 1999 World Cup is by far not the only great tournament to date. Each one has been special in its own way, each with excitement, drama, goals, and star players. As a result, women's soccer has grown substantially around the world. As teams move forward, creating new epochs to look back on, new stories will be written as new players embark on a quest for greatness with the end goal being the elusive World Cup trophy.

France 2019 represents the most recent chapter in this ongoing story, one told in the form of books, newspapers, magazines, TV features, and film documentaries, one with a special catalogue of winners and host nations, along with intricate details of the players and coaches that make the World Cup go round. Every four years, a new tournament is not only capturing a piece of women's soccer history, but it's also capturing a part of world history.

AUTHOR'S NOTE

The "Overall Team Ranking" is different from the "FIFA Ranking Going Into the World Cup." The former is the ranking I gave each team based on each country's history in the World Cup, recent performances, star players, and FIFA ranking. The latter was a ranking that FIFA assigned each team prior to the 2019 World Cup and listed on its website.

This book was published as close to the 2019 FIFA Women's World Cup as possible, and all information was up to date upon publication. Some players, and even coaches for that matter, might have changed in the small time period between finishing this book and the actual World Cup kicking off in France. That's a fact of life in sports: teams change, players change, lineups shift around.

A great deal of thanks is given to the people behind the sources provided within. Thanks to everyone at Meyer & Meyer Sport and Cardinal Publishers Group. Thanks also to my mom and everyone else who has helped along the way.

ENDNOTES

1 Andrew Keh, *"U.S. Draws Sweden, Thailand and Chile at 2019 Women's World Cup,"* The New York Times, published December 8, 2018, accessed January 11, 2019, https://www.nytimes.com/2018/12/08/sports/womens-world-cup-draw.html

2 Andrew Das, *"U.S. Soccer Team Maps Out Six-Month Schedule Ahead of Women's World Cup,"* The New York Times, published December 6, 2018, accessed January 11, 2019, https://www.nytimes.com/2018/12/06/sports/soccer-world-cup-women-united-states.html

3 Steven Goff, "U.S. women's soccer team will take on tough schedule before World Cup," *The Washington Post*, published December 6, 2018, accessed January 11, 2019, https://www.washingtonpost.com/sports/2018/12/06/us-womens-soccer-team-will-take-tough-schedule-before-world-cup/?noredirect=on&utm_term=.ded0e6e5437a

4 Nick Carbone, "A FAMILY AFFAIR Adidas vs. Puma," *TIME*, published August 23, 2011, accessed February 7, 2019, http://content.time.com/time/specials/packages/article/0,28804,2089859_2089888_2089889,00.html

5 "Jones sacked as Germany coach," FIFA.com, published March 13, 2018, accessed January 26, 2018, https://www.fifa.com/womensworldcup/news/jones-sacked-as-germany-coach

6 "FIFA Women's World Cup France 2019 [Germany]," FIFA.com, accessed February 7, 2019, https://www.fifa.com/womensworldcup/teams/team/1882879/profile/

7 Dorothy Wickenden, "Kai-Fu Lee on China's Race to the Future," *The New Yorker*, published January 28, 2019, accessed January 29, 2019, https://www.newyorker.com/podcast/political-scene/kai-fu-lee-on-chinas-race-to-the-future

8 Luisita Lopez Torregrosa, "What to See and Do in Spain," *The New York Times*, published January 16, 2018, accessed January 29, 2018, https://www.nytimes.com/2018/01/16/travel/spain-travel-guide.html

9 *Wikipedia, The Free Encyclopedia*, s.vv. "Scotland women's national football team," accessed January 20, 2019, https://en.wikipedia.org/wiki/Scotland_women%27s_national_football_team

10 (CNN), "What is VAR? The Video Assistant Referee explained," *CNN.com*, updated June 19, 2018, accessed January 31, 2019, https://www.cnn.com/2018/06/19/sport/var-video-assistant-referee-world-cup-russia-2018-int-spt/index.html

11 R.E. | MEXICO CITY, The Economist explains, "Why Mexico's murder rate is soaring," *The Economist*, published May 9 2018, accessed January 27, 2019, https://www.economist.com/the-economist-explains/2018/05/09/why-mexicos-murder-rate-is-soaring

THE Women's World Cup 2019 Book

CREDITS

Design & Layout
Cover and interior design: Annika Naas
Layout: Zerosoft
Cover and interior photos: © dpa, picture-alliance.com

Editorial
Managing editor: Elizabeth Evans

MORE GREAT BOOKS

EUROPEAN SOCCER LEAGUES 2019

EVERYTHING YOU NEED TO KNOW ABOUT THE 2019/20 SEASON

336 p., b/w
7 photos + illus.
Paperback, 5.5 x 8.5"
ISBN: 978-1-78255-175-1
$14.95 US

This book gives every fan an all-access look into Europe's storied club teams, including the players, coaches, each team's style of play, their future direction, along with background on key stadiums and cities. All of the legendary leagues, teams, and players are featured. For generations, fans have established their place behind their teams, based on a passionate love affair with their chosen jersey and the long history it stands for. This book takes the fan through every aspect of the upcoming European club season, featuring the million-dollar talent from Real Madrid to Manchester United and illuminating the very best of European soccer.

BY SHANE STAY

MAJOR LEAGUE SOCCER 2019

EVERYTHING YOU NEED TO KNOW ABOUT THE TEAMS

336 p., b/w
7 photos + illus.
Paperback, 5.5 x 8.5"
ISBN: 978-1-78255-159-1
$14.95 US

Major League Soccer (MLS) is on the fast track to becoming the world's next super league. This book gives in-depth information on this amazing league, including the players, coaches, each team's style of play, and even background on each MLS city. MLS is a league that has attracted the world's best, such as David Beckham and Wayne Rooney, along with a host of talent from the United States men's national soccer team, including Landon Donovan and Clint Dempsey. All the players and current team rosters are discussed in this book. While players come and go, the fans are beginning to establish an unbreakable, lifelong bond with their teams, and this book will spur their enthusiasm.

MEYER & MEYER Sport
Von-Coels-Str. 390
52080 Aachen
Germany

Phone +49 02 41 - 9 58 10 - 13
Fax +49 02 41 - 9 58 10 - 10
E-Mail sales@m-m-sports.com
Website www. thesportspublisher.com

All books available as E-books.

MEYER
& MEYER
SPORT